A Thousand Battles

An Intelligence Officer's Battle Behind Enemy Lines in Wartime Burma

Serena Merton

Helion & Company Limited

In loving memory of cousins Robin and Zienia Merton

Helion & Company Limited
Unit 8 Amherst Business Centre
Budbrooke Road
Warwick
CV34 5WE
England
Tel. 01926 499 619
Email: info@helion.co.uk
Website: www.helion.co.uk
Twitter: @helionbooks
Visit our blog at blog.helion.co.uk

Published by Helion & Company 2021
Designed and typeset by Mach 3 Solutions Ltd (www.mach3solutions.co.uk)
Cover designed by Paul Hewitt, Battlefield Design (www.battlefield-design.co.uk)

ISBN 978-1-914377-41-9

British Library Cataloguing-in-Publication Data.
A catalogue record for this book is available from the British Library.

Contents

Acknowledgements

I would first and foremost like to thank Jilly Merton for the protracted loan of papers and books belonging to the late Robin Merton, who was the most thorough and dogged researcher and keeper of family history – I so wish he were here to offer my thanks. And though I cannot thank her personally, I'm so grateful to the late Zienia Merton for her permission to research her father's life and wartime experiences.

I am grateful to Tracey Blodgett of Lakefield College, Ontario, Paul Jordan of Eastbourne College, Sally Kent of Cambridge University and Clare Butlin of Clare College, Cambridge for delving into their archives on my behalf.

The research staff at the Imperial War Museum who were, as always, helpful, efficient and courteous and allowed me extra time to study the extensive papers of Cecil Merton.

I am most grateful to Bertie Lawson, the Managing Director of Sampan Travel in Yangon, who has been most long suffering, putting up with my requests for assistance in Myanmar.

With grateful thanks to Duncan Rogers, Dr Michael LoCicero, George Anderson and Kim McSweeney of Helion & Company for their guidance and to James Kerr who photographed the hundred-year-old albums of Walter Merton.

Abbreviations

ALFSEA	Allied Land Forces South East Asia
AVG	American Volunteer Group
BURCORPS	Burma Corps
BFF	Burma Frontier Force
BMA	Burmese National Army
BURDIV	Burma Division
BURIF	Burma Rifles
BURWING	RAF Burma
CGS	Chief of the General Staff
LAA	Light Anti-Aircraft
LCT	Landing Craft, Tank
L of C	Line of Command
LMG	Light Machine Gun

Burmese Honorifics

Maung	Boy or young man – "Young Brother"
Ma	Girl or young woman – "Young Sister"
Ko	Older man – "Elder Brother"
Daw	Married or elder woman
U	Respected elder man
Bo	Army officer

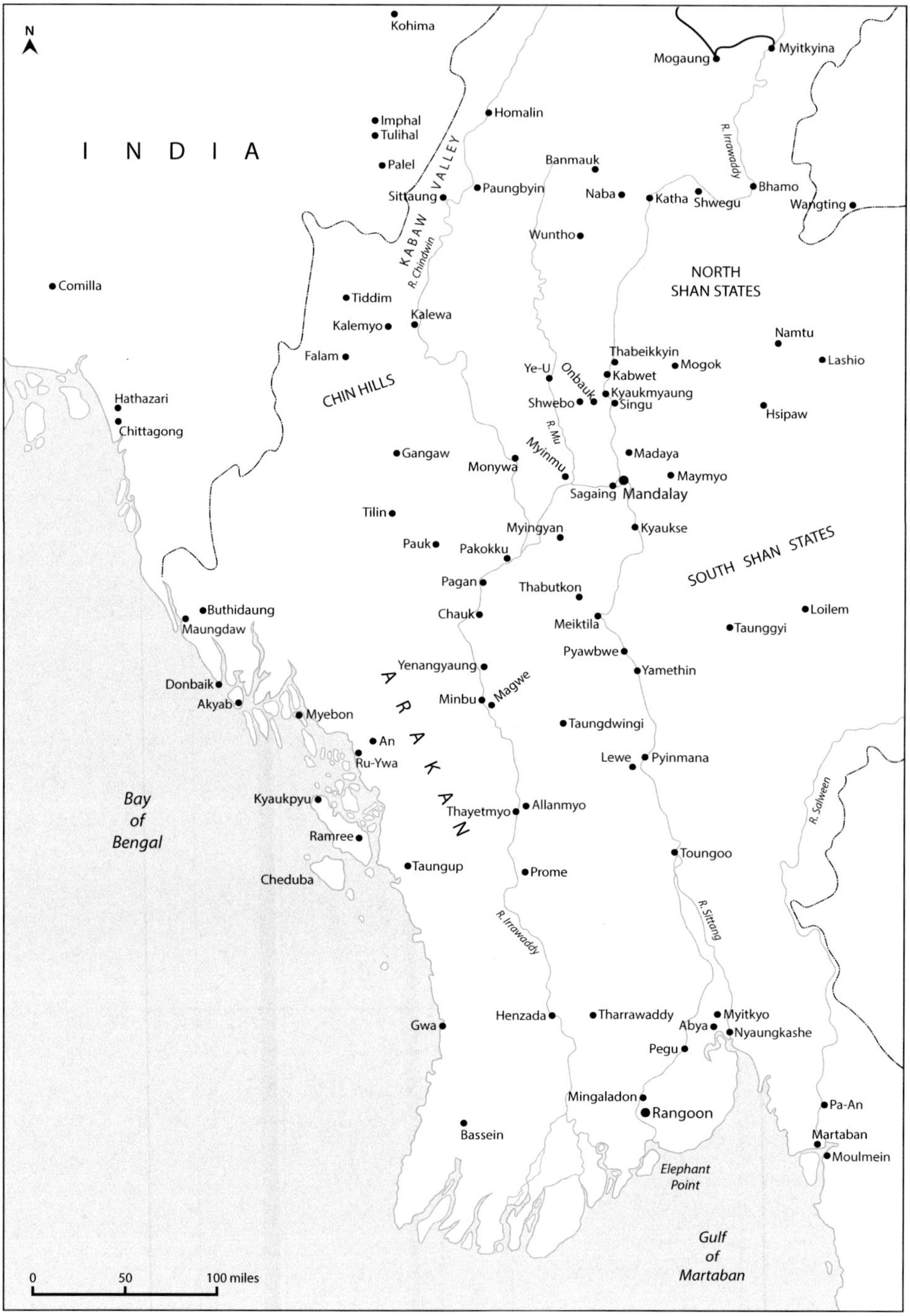
N
Kohima
Mogaung
Myitkyina
Homalin
Imphal
Tulihal
I N D I A
R. Irrawaddy
Palel
KABAW VALLEY
Banmauk
Bhamo
Sittaung
Paungbyin
Naba
Katha
Shwegu
Wangting
Wuntho
R. Chindwin
Comilla
NORTH SHAN STATES
Tiddim
Kalewa
Kalemyo
Namtu
Falam
Thabeikkyin
Lashio
Ye-U
Onbauk
Kabwet
Mogok
CHIN HILLS
Kyaukmyaung
Hathazari
Shwebo
Singu
Hsipaw
Chittagong
R. Mu
Gangaw
Myinmu
Madaya
Monywa
Maymyo
Sagaing
Mandalay
Tilin
Myingyan
Kyaukse
Pauk
Pakokku
SOUTH SHAN STATES
Pagan
Thabutkon
Buthidaung
Chauk
Loilem
Maungdaw
Meiktila
Taunggyi
Pyawbwe
Yenangyaung
Yamethin
Donbaik
Minbu
Magwe
Akyab
Myebon
Taungdwingi
An
Lewe
Pyinmana
Ru-Ywa
A R A K A N
R. Salween
Bay of Bengal
Kyaukpyu
Allanmyo
Thayetmyo
Ramree
Toungoo
Taungup
Prome
Cheduba
R. Sittang
R. Irrawaddy
Henzada
Tharrawaddy
Myitkyo
Gwa
Abya
Nyaungkashe
Pegu
Mingaladon
Pa-An
Rangoon
Bassein
Martaban
Moulmein
Elephant Point
Gulf of Martaban
0
50
100 miles

Burma 1939.

1

"A Thousand Battles, A Thousand Victories"

'Know thy self, know thy enemy. A thousand battles, a thousand victories'.[1] The military strategist Sun Tzu writing in 5th century BC China understood that the fight against the enemy is just one of many battles within a conflict. The jungles and highlands of Burma provided as many, if not more, hardships for the men of Z Force than the Japanese enemy did during their three-year occupation. An unforgiving terrain, rivers up to a mile wide, dysentery, cholera, malarial mosquitoes; monsoon rains, mites, skin diseases, jungle typhus, ticks, leeches, heat, humidity, hunger; thirst, murderous *dacoits*, traitorous tribesmen as well as the cruellest of enemies occupied their daily lives. There was also an internal battle raging in the mind of Cecil Merton; not knowing if his wife and children had survived the 'one thousand and eighty-seven days of separation and suspense, wondering if we would ever find each other alive again.'[2]

Cecil Gerald Merton (known as Micky) was born on 5 March 1908 in Salmon Arm, British Columbia, the third and youngest child of Gerald R Merton and his Swiss wife, Lily Boy-de-la-Tour, who had met and married in New Westminster, British Columbia in 1903. Gerald had emigrated to Canada and bought a farm in the rich fruit growing area of Shuswap county. Salmon Arm became a city on 15 May 1905 having attracted fruit farmers to the area from 1904 onwards. The Farmer's Institute sponsored exhibitions at Kamloops and New Westminster to attract farmers and the Hudson's Bay Company displayed local produce in its shop window in Vancouver.

1 Sun Tzu, *The Art of War.*
2 Memoirs/papers of C G Merton Imperial War Museum (IWM)/05/11/1.

Gerald Merton. (Family Archive)

Merton children. (Family Archive)

So numerous were the British farmers arriving at this time and 'English expatriates stuck together trying to approximate life in the Old Country as closely as possible. So many homed in on South Canoe it was soon dubbed 'Little England' by the other half.'[3]

Lady Elcho, writing to her husband said '(If) I were a man, I'd settle there and buy a fruit farm – in fact if I'd any capital, I'd buy a small valley right away.'[4]

Gerald and Lily made their home at Merton House,[5] a large timbered house on Merton Hill in the lush valley of Salmon Arm, named after the large runs of salmon in the South Western arm of Shuswap Lake.

Renée Maud was born in Switzerland but Walter Hugh and Cecil Gerald were born in British Columbia completing the family. British Columbia provided the growing children with an outdoor, adventurous, sporting life including skiing, skating and ice hockey during the winter months. Cecil's passion for shooting and fishing was established there. The family returned

3 *Salmon Arm: A Short History* <www.salmonarm.ca>
4 Lady Elcho to Lord Elcho, 2 March 1909, Stanway papers.
5 Now numbered 1371 Merton Hill.

Walter and Cecil. (Family Archive)

Walter and Cecil. (Family Archive)

Merton House 1907. (Family Archive)

Odelboden. (Family Archive)

Gerald and Lily. (Family Archive)

Gerald, Lily, Renée and Cecil Merton. (Family Archive)

home to the United Kingdom for a long visit from December 1912 on *Caronia* from New York to Liverpool returning on the *Royal George* from Bristol to Montreal in August 1913.

In 1914 Walter became a pupil at Lakefield Preparatory School in Ontario and was joined by Cecil three years later. The school, which was founded in 1879 by Sparham Sheldrake as The Grove Preparatory School (school fees were $60 a quarter) was bought in 1895 by the Reverend Doctor Alexander Mackenzie and was renamed Lakefield, providing boys with a well-rounded and rigorous education of academia, the arts, sports and outdoor activities. It was over two thousand miles from Salmon Arm to Lakefield, a journey undertaken on the Canadian Pacific Railway which had allowed British Columbia to join the rest of Canada and opened up the vast country.

Walter was reaching the age when he was to start his public school education and the family left Canada for good in April 1919 on *Tunisian* bound from St John's to Liverpool when Cecil was 10 years old. They were to make their home at White Ladies, Beaconsfield as well as 15 Queen's Gate in London. Senior schooling was awaiting Cecil and he followed his elder brother to Eastbourne College in 1921. They were both members of Gonville boarding house. Walter was a fraternal hard-act to follow being a School Prefect, Head of House, Company Sergeant Major in College Corps as well as a member of the First XV for two years running winning him the important appellation 'Stag' referring to the stag on the 1st XV kit and cap.[6] Cecil also soon excelled at school being made a School Prefect, Head of House, Company Sergeant in College Corps and a member of the First XV in '24, '25, '26 and '27 as well as being in the 2nd Swimming team in 1927. He passed his certificate with an A grade enabling him to gain a place at Cambridge

On 1 November 1927 Cecil matriculated at Clare College, Cambridge where he was reading Agriculture, Estate Management and Forestry. During his three years at Cambridge, he represented the University at skiing and he graduated on 21 June 1930.[7] His original plan was to join the Colonial Service but this involved a year's post-graduate course at Oxford and, impatient to get on with life, he abandoned that plan and embarked from Liverpool on

6 The stag forms part of the coat of arms of the Duke of Devonshire, the school patron.
7 UA Graduate 12/160, Sally Kent, Archivist.

CGM at Eastbourne College 1927.
(Eastbourne College Archives)

CGM in Eastbourne College First XI Rugby Team. (Eastbourne College Archives)

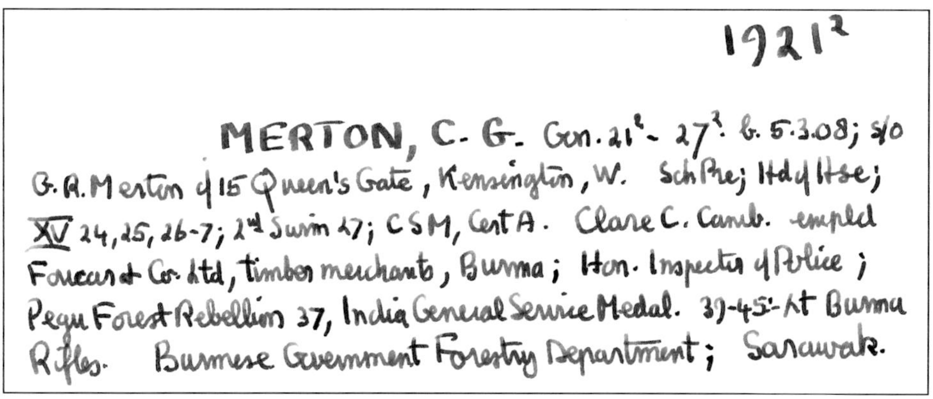

1921²

MERTON, C. G. Gon. 21² - 27³. b. 5.3.08; s/o G. A. Merton of 15 Queen's Gate, Kensington, W. Sch Pre; Hd of Hse; XV 24, 25, 26-7; 2nd Swim 27; CSM, Cert A. Clare C. Camb. empld Foucar & Co. Ltd, timber merchants, Burma; Hon. Inspector of Police; Pegu Forest Rebellion 37, India General Service Medal. 39-45: Lt Burma Rifles. Burmese Government Forestry Department; Sarawak.

CGM in Eastbourne Archives (Eastbourne College Archives)

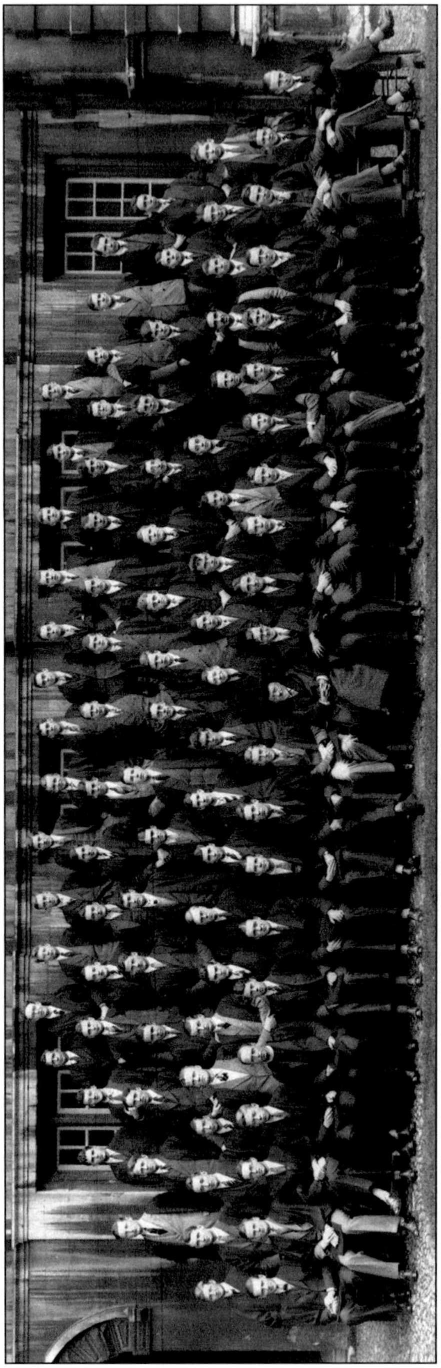

Matriculation at Clare College, Cambridge 1927. (Clare College Archives)

Shropshire disembarking in Rangoon on 3 October 1930 to start his employment with Messrs Foucar & Company[8] as an Assistant Forestry Manager.

Life for an Assistant Forestry Manager was tough, nomadic and not for the faint hearted. He lived in the jungle with a cook, houseboy and wash boy in a spacious bamboo house which took three weeks to build but would last for a year before another was needed to be built.

CGM at Cambridge. (Family Archives)

The Burma Government Forest Department controlled all the Burmese forests; these were divided into seven Circles and each Circle contained four or five Divisions. A Division covered thousands of square miles and a Divisional Forest Officer administered to each with Assistant Forestry Managers assisting him. Their roles included recruitment of staff; administering welfare and discipline to the rangers, *oozos* (elephant drivers) and their elephants; allotting leases to contractors; building and repair of forest tracks; acting as game wardens issuing shooting licences and controlling poaching. The Divisional staff knew their forests intimately making the need for maps superfluous.

Within a year he was to meet and marry Minny, the daughter of U Tun Win,[9] Superintendent (officiating) of Land Records[10] from Minbu, near

8 One of the largest timber companies in Burma at that time, founded in 1878 in Moulmein by Ferdinand Louis Foucar and joined by his brother E J Foucar in 1880. Ferdinand died in 1899 and the company became an LLC with E J Foucar as Senior Managing Director. It employed 4,000-5,000 Burmese and 300-400 elephants.

9 U is an honorific for a respected elder.

10 *Thacker's Directory for Minbu 1931*, Anglo Burmese Library Archives.

Bamboo hut. (Lieutenant General Sir Geoffrey Evans)

Lunch at the Katha Club. Far left, Cecil Merton; seated fifth from left, F V Webster; standing behind Webster, J K Parry; seated third from right, Minny Merton; standing behind, H E Castens. (Lieutenant General Sir Geoffrey Evans)

Magway in Central Burma. For seven years Cecil and Minny lived this peripatetic life and Minny would accompany her husband on his tours around the forests. She shared Cecil's love of fishing although it did have its dangerous moments. Once she was charged by a wild elephant and she scrambled up a tall tree where she sat for hours in the treetop until it eventually ambled away. Jungle life was interspersed with a month's leave every year and a long leave every fourth year.

The arrival of daughters, June on 4 July 1932 and Fiona on 12 November 1937 did not alter their nomadic, jungle life at first but before long the need for an education meant a more sedentary lifestyle and they bought five acres and built a bungalow in Aniskan village, five miles from Maymyo (now known as Pyin Oo Lwin) and settled into a more static, conventional family life. This was expected to be their home for their future retirement in Burma but outside forces were evolving to change their lives forever.

2

War

> "War doesn't negate decency; it demands it, even more than in times of peace."
>
> Khaled Husseini, *The Kite Runner*

At the outbreak of the war in Europe, Cecil was on leave in the United Kingdom and he immediately applied to join the Artists Rifles but he was turned down once he revealed his current occupation, his knowledge of the country and his linguistic abilities. It was suggested that he would be more use in Burma so he returned to his job for a further year. He tried once again to join up, this time the Navy, but was again turned down for the same reasons. His persistence paid off, being sent to an Officer Cadet Training Unit[1] and offered a temporary commission in 2 Burma Infantry Brigade in Moulmein. Before departure, he made arrangements for Minny and the children's evacuation to India in case of an invasion that was never expected to happen.

James Lunt writes 'A Cadet Training Unit was established in Maymyo. The young men who passed through it could well be described as the cream of young Britain. They were junior members of the Civil Service and Police, employees of the great teak firms ('Teak Wallahs'), the Burma Oil Company, the commercial houses and the Irrawaddy Flotilla Company. Many were university graduates. Almost all spoke the language, and most were accustomed to lead people of other races. Many were inured to the loneliness of the jungle when extracting teak, all were used to responsibility … and many

1 Course number 27/4 28 April 1941 in Maymyo.

HQ 2 Burma Brigade. Left to right: Lieutenant W Cruikshank, Major S J H Green, Brigadier A J H Bourke and Captain C G Merton. (James Lunt)

were decorated for bravery in the course of the war. They made outstanding officers.'[2]

With his extensive knowledge of the language and the lie of the land, he was appointed their Intelligence Officer (and Mess Secretary). This small garrison was the Headquarters of Tenasserim Area and consisted of a Brigadier, John

2 Lunt, J D, *The Burma Rifles: Journal of the Society for Army Historical Research,* Vol.76, No.307.

Bourke,[3] a Brigade Major, Charles Appleby,[4] Staff Captain James Lunt and Cecil as Intelligence Officer. Warrant Officers, Liason Officer and the Chief Clerk completed the Headquarters Tenasserim Area which was re-designated Headquarters 2 Burma Brigade in November 1941. A state of emergency was imminent and all leave was cancelled and men recalled.

Lunt described Cecil's relationship with Appleby as fairly fractious. 'He [Cecil] seldom saw eye to eye with Appleby and carried on an amicable feud with the Brigadier whose taste in food frequently ran counter to Merton's own … speaking fluent Burmese, completely unperturbable, he found the ways of the Regular army beyond all understanding … My only complaint against him was that he smoked the strongest-smelling Burmese cheroots. Other than that, he was brave, humorous, a wonderful companion and the nicest man one could hope to meet.'[5]

Moulmein (now known as Mawlamyine) is situated on the east bank of the River Salween and was Burma's third largest port, over looked by the Kyaik Than Lan Pagoda, made famous by Kipling. Martaban, on the opposite bank, was Moulmein's railhead for trains to Rangoon. It was surrounded firstly by paddy fields, then rolling hills covered in scrub and beyond that the jungle-clad hills.

'Hindsight makes the writing of history easy (if inaccurate), but I do not think that most of us serving in Burma at that time anticipated attack by the Japanese'[6] wrote James Lunt[7] who served with Cecil in 2 Burma Rifles (commonly known as BURIFS). Burma was considered a backwater where the world war was concerned; Lunt describes 'our intelligence regarding the Japanese was lamentable. In a comment on the lack of Intelligence organization in Burma, the War Office was later moved to comment: 'This lack was not peculiar to Burma. It is fair to say that throughout the British Empire the necessity for an Intelligence Service was realised by Service Headquarters but the various Governments concerned were not prepared to spend the money

3 Brigadier A J H Bourke, Connaught Rangers, Guides Infantry, 92 Punjabis (8th Punjab Regiment).

4 Major Charles Appleby DSO later commanded 2/1 Punjabis. DSO gazette 13.09.45.

5 Lunt, James, *The Retreat from Burma 1941-1942* (Newton Abbot: David & Charles Publishers, 1986), p.75.

6 Ibid, p. 73.

7 Major General James Lunt, 1917-2001, formerly The Duke of Wellington's Regiment, 4th Burma Rifles, 16/5th Lancers.

to make it effective.'[8] Even as late in the war as 1944 General Slim's 'huge problem was intelligence', and he complained to XI Army Group on 23 June that he was 'blind'.[9]

Officers of 2 BURIF were of the opinion that if the Japanese war machine invaded Burma it would be through the Northern Shan States, cutting across the Burma Road but in October 1941, General McLeod[10] informed the assembled officers that war with Japan was anticipated, that the Japanese force would be overwhelming and no reinforcements would be available. Their role would be merely to delay the advance not to survive it.

The attack on Pearl Harbour on 7 December 1941 led to the United States declaration of war against Imperial Japan on 8 December and the Japanese wasted no time invading Thailand, Malaya, Hong Kong and the Philippines. On 15 December a cable was sent from the General Staff in New Delhi to the Chiefs of Staff in London with recommendations for Burma's defence; increasing the air force in Burma; increasing defence on all border crossings from Thailand; mobilization of guerrilla forces; movement of two divisions from India to Burma; and a step up of communications with China.

Commander-in-Chief Wavell[11] arrived in Rangoon on 21 December for meetings with General McLeod and Sir Reginald Dorman-Smith[12] before setting off for Chungking for a meeting with Chiang Kai-Shek. Chiang offered to dispatch his Fifth and Sixth armies to Burma. Wavell accepted the Sixth Army which was already on the border of Burma and Yunnan. Criticised for not accepting more help, he was fearful of Chinese empirical ambitions in Northern Burma and unsure of their fighting ability. Wavell's return to India was high on drama with his plane losing its way, landing in Moulmein and then taking off again for Mingalodon, landing there just ahead of Japanese planes bombing Rangoon. Cecil's own notes state that 'there was no warning that Japan would invade Burma.'[13]

8 Ibid., p.61.
9 Duckett, Richard, *The Special Operations Executive in Burma* (London: Bloomsbury Academic, 2017), p.11.
10 Major General D K McLeod (1885-1958), GOC Burma, formerly Guides Cavalry.
11 Field Marshall Sir Archibald Percival Wavell MC (1883-1950).
12 Sir Reginald Hugh Dorman-Smith (1899-1977), Governor of Burma from 6 May 1941 to 31 August 1946.
13 Memoirs/papers of C G Merton, IWM/05/11/1.

3

Retreat

"If I have seen further, it is by standing on the shoulders of giants."
Sir Isaac Newton

Heavy air raids on Rangoon during 23-25 December gave a dramatic hint as to what would follow. The city was defended by the P-40B Tomahawks and Buffaloes of the RAF and the AVG but successive waves of Japanese bombers[1] flying in tight formation from airfields in Thailand and Indo-China, escorted by fighters,[2] set the city ablaze. With wooden buildings bombed and burning, a breakdown of law and order and panic started amongst the Indian population upon whom the city was dependent on for all its needs. The dockworkers, porters and household staff abandoned their jobs and started the long trek north to India, on foot or in bullock carts. Docked ships were left unloaded becoming sitting targets for the Japanese bombers. *Lu-zos* (criminals) targeted the fleeing Indians as well as the undefended homes in the city. Zoo keepers had abandoned their post and dangerous animals in the zoo were killed for their meat and other harmless creatures were released into the wild. Criminals were released from jail and lunatics from their asylums.

The Indian exodus took two major routes; the northern route up the Irrawaddy via Prome and finally over the mountains into Manipur state or the shorter Eastern route over the Arakan *Yomas* (hills) and north towards Chittagong. Roads were clogged with hundreds of thousands of bedraggled travellers. Heat exhaustion, malaria, cholera, dehydration, smallpox and in some cases, wild

1 Mitsubishi Ki-21 Heavy Bombers – twin engines carrying a 2200lb bomb load.
2 Nakajima Ki-27 Interceptor Fighter-Bombers.

animals, sealed the fate of many. The streaming lines of refugees were up to thirty miles long and they were fed by the generosity of Burmese villagers, tea planters and the army who set up encampments *en route*. There were food dumps at regular distances to feed the thousands. Cecil notes 'Camps organised and encouragement to return to work (free transport).'[3] Many climbed on top of packed trains and a number were killed, unaware of the low railway bridges. Cecil's handwritten notes state 'Second raid – mass exodus! 500,000 people, 300,000 Indians'[4] on the move. It is estimated that between 50,000 and 100,000 civilians died on their trek out of Burma.

Soon the British government officials, teak wallahs and merchants were to begin their own flights. In the early days there was an air evacuation but this was shut down by 9 May. Flights for India were taking off from Myitkyina and there was a frantic scramble to get there in time before flights ceased. Families crowded onto available steamers up river and those that left their departure too late, also started the long trek north on foot or by bullock cart.

In Moulmein, the Headquarters of 2 Burma Infantry Brigade had become part of the 17th Division commanded by Major-General Jackie Smyth,[5] awarded the VC at Festubert and the MC in the North-West Frontier when he was also recommended for a bar to his VC. Lunt describes him as a 'bright, perky and friendly little man, with a wonderful ability to put young officers like me at their ease' but he was also considered 'too ambitious, and something of a showman'.[6] He was not a well man; suffering from an anal fissure, malaria and previously hospitalised in Quetta where he was operated on for an internal abscess; the wound burst open upon evacuation from the hospital after an earthquake.

His own description of the line of communication was 'The long line of communications from Moulmein northwards towards Bilin and Sittang … was an absolute nightmare … from Moulmein northwards there was a somewhat antiquated steamer ferry service over the 7,000 yards of open water which lay between Moulmein and Martaban, a good metal road and a single track

3 Memoirs/papers of C G Merton IWM/05/11/1.
4 Ibid.
5 Major General Sir John G Smythe VC (Festubert May 1915) MC (1893-1983), 15th Ludhiana Sikhs.
6 Lunt, James, *op.cit.*, p.107.

railway ran back through Thaton over the Bilin Road to Kyaikto. Thence a dusty unmade track led to the Sittang river railway bridge'.[7]

As the crow flies, the Gulf of Martaban in the Andaman Sea separates Moulmein from Rangoon but overland there are three major river systems to negotiate; the tidal Salween River with the antiquated ferry service, then fifty miles north is the Bilin River which rises in the Karenni Hills and exits into the sea at the Gulf of Martaban. A further fifty miles north is the River Sittang which rises on the Shan Plateau near the town of Yamethin and also exits into the Gulf of Martaban. The railway bridge on the Sittang was single tracked and half a mile long. It was unusable by vehicles so there were a couple of basic ferries above the bridge for vehicular and foot crossings.

Smyth was convinced that the Sittang was the best place to defend Rangoon from the Japanese but he was overruled by his superior Lieutenant General Hutton[8] as well as Wavell and the Governor. Smyth wrote to Maurice Collins in 1955 'It was the Governor of Burma who was so strongly against my plan to concentrate behind the Sittang because it would have brought the Japanese so close to Rangoon that it would have fatally weakened the morale of the people of Burma'.[9]

On 20 January, the first Japanese troops crossed over the Thai-Burmese border at Mayawaddy and Palu[10] and had taken Tavoy. Communication was very haphazard and confusion ruled but Lunt notes in his diary that 'News very bad. Japs have broken through at Kawkareik. 16 Brigade burnt all their equipment … 17 Div are clearing out their HQ… burnt all our documents etc … state of chaos in Moulmein. Higher command still deciding whether to hang on to the place or not. They still say it is to be a 'second Tobruk'!'[11]

On 23 January Smyth's Divisional Headquarters moved from Moulmein to Kyaikto, leaving the BURIFS behind for the time being. 'No one, including the Brigadier, knows whether we are to stay here, or to follow HQ 17 Div. Yesterday we were leaving; today, it seems we are staying' wrote Lunt in his diary'.[12] Rumours were rife and 2 Burma Brigade were frantically attempting to put Moulmein into a belated state of defence.

7 Smythe, Sir John, *Before the Dawn* (London: Cassell, 1957), p.140.
8 Lieutenant General Thomas J Hutton, GOC Burma Army (1890-1981).
9 Smythe papers IWM.
10 55th Japanese Infantry Division.
11 Lunt, James, *op.cit.*, p.107.
12 Ibid., p.100.

Cecil and Lunt got into trouble with Appleby when he overheard them discussing their chances of getting out of Moulmein alive and Appleby accused them of being defeatist and placed them under arrest. They both had work to do but were made to stay put until a guard could escort them to Brigade Headquarters. The Brigadier was livid that he had been unable to find Lunt and Cecil because, by now, Appleby had collapsed from nervous exhaustion and Lunt was needed to take over until the new Brigade Major L G Wheeler arrived from 3 BURIF.

Lunt writes in his diary on 30 January 'Merton wakes me about 0100 hours. Says he thinks he can hear firing. Most extraordinary 'whooping' noise, which we can't place. Also, the continuous howling of starving pi-dogs. We get dressed and lie down clothed. About 0700 hours heavy firing from Zegyo; Japs had tried to rush through 8 BURIF LMG [light machine gun] post in some of our own 30 cwt lorries which they presumably captured at Kawkareik. No time for breakfast so hurry over to Brigade HQ. Everyone very worried and L G Wheeler tells me there is Jap attack on aerodrome. 12 Mountain Battery are firing; main attack seems around Zegyo. Watts who is commanding Kokine detachment on aerodrome is directing fire. Japs have him surrounded by midday. Heavy firing all the morning; 8 BURIF are steady but 3 BURIF are shaky'.[13] Cecil is bit less voluble in his diary, '30 Jan: Japs attack Moulmein. 31 Jan: Moulmein falls?'[14]

Withdrawal began at 0800 hours on the 31 January with the Japanese controlling most of the north of the town. Lunt's diary tells us 'Decision taken at 0400 hours to evacuate at daylight … terrific fires in the bazaar. Evacuation at daylight from Kaladan, North and Mission Street Jetties. Bayonet charge at daylight in Salween Park, led by 'Bonzo' Bowers [OC 8 Burma Rifles]. Evacuation completed by 0830 hours. Brigade Headquarters leaves last. Large force of bombers passed over while we waited on the jetty. No bombs fortunately. Japs already on South Jetty before we leave. Crossing very slow. Shelled the whole way over by Jap guns from Battery Point. Most uncomfortable. Crossing took about 50 minutes. On arrival in Martaban there was chaos. The Japs were shelling trains and causing casualties … eventually got away in train

13 Ibid., p.112.
14 Memoirs/papers of C G Merton IWM/05/11/1.

about 1200 hours. Meet Brigadier in Thaton who sends me to Kyaito … dog tired.'[15]

2 Burma Brigade had left most of their possessions behind in Moulmein and had arrived in Kyaikto unshaven and in some cases, shirtless. They had only just settled in when they were ordered to move once more to Nyaunglebin where they were in charge of a fifty mile stretch of the Sittang River from above the Sittang bridge to Schwegyin. They arrived by train on 15 February, days after the Japanese 33rd Division[16] had crossed into Burma near Pa-an on the River Salween north of Moulmein. This small market town was so quiet and unaffected by war that Cecil decided to get Minny down from Maymyo for a few days. Much against the Brigade Major's advice, Minny arrived by train five days later by which time circumstances had changed dramatically and she stayed for a week and then had to return north.

At Nyaunglebin, 2 Burma Brigade were miles north of the Sittang Bridge with limited communications and little transport. Brigadier Bourke took Cecil on a reconnaissance of the bridge on 19 February. They met with Smyth and Bourke remonstrated vociferously that if they were to be expected to defend from the bridge to Nyaunglebin, they urgently needed more troops.

Smyth and the 17th Division were now fighting a desperate four-day battle on the River Bilin to check the enemy's advance north until Smyth pulled his troops back from Bilin to the Sittang. Unfortunately, the Japanese intercepted an un-coded message about their withdrawal and Lieutenant General Sakurai ordered his 215 Infantry Regiment to outflank Smyth on the left through the jungle using hidden paths, to try and seize the bridge at Sittang ahead of him.

Friendly fire from the RAF and AVG as well as enemy fire from Japanese planes onto the congested roads added to the chaos as well as a lack of communication with Rangoon. Boats and transport were set on fire, roads were congested; hunger, thirst and confusion ruled. With limited communication the battle raged all night long.

Smyth appointed Brigadier Hugh-Jones[17] to be in charge of the bridge defences, whilst he moved his Headquarters west to Abya where there was a better chance of telephone communication with Rangoon as the wireless

15 Lunt, James, *op.cit.*, p.115.
16 33rd Division commanded by Lieutenant General Seizo Sakurai (1889-1985).
17 Brigadier Noel Hugh-Jones MC (1894-1952), Royal Welsh Fusiliers, 53rd Sikhs, 48th Gurkha Brigade.

sets did not work in poor climactic conditions. With him eight miles away and Wavell two thousand miles away in Java, the decision was finally given to destroy the bridge. This was done at 0530 on 23 February. 'A terrible decision had to be made by Smyth,' wrote General Davies. 'If he blew the bridge, he sacrificed the bulk of his division. If he failed to blow the bridge and it was secured intact by the enemy, the way to Rangoon lay open with nothing interposing. General Smyth blew the bridge. In my opinion a heroic and inevitable decision.'[18] This controversial decision was to be argued over for years to come and took its final casualty in 1952 when Hugh-Jones walked out into the sea for one final time at East Preston.

In Nyaunglebin, the news of the Sittang Disaster did not filter through until 25 February when a visiting officer of 17th Division informed the disbelieving Headquarters. They were also incredulous of the huge caravans of refugees crawling through the town; streams and streams of vehicles passing through along with the pedestrians carrying their meagre belongings. Their number was increased by soldiers limping in from the Sittang battle on foot or on trains.

On 28 February, 2 Burma Brigade joined 1 BURDIV and left Nyaunglebin for Toungoo[19] only to find it a burning ruin. The roads were still blocked by streams of refugees and travel was slow and choked. 'Thousands of refugees in cars, buses, on bullock carts and on foot are streaming through. Chaos reigns supreme. The entire town is evacuating. Pathetic scenes at station where people struggle to board trains'.[20]

Cecil was worried about Minny having not heard anything from her since he put her on a train from Nyaunglebin; he had good reason to worry hearing the rumours that the Japanese were arresting women and interning them in camps. There were also rumours that women were being taken off ships heading for Calcutta and their names were being broadcast on Radio Saigon; the definitive psychological warfare. 'Merton was just plain gloomy, worried to death about his wife and children, hating the army and its idiotic ways' wrote Lunt in his diary.[21]

18 Lunt, James, *op.cit.*, p.143 quoting letter from Cowan to Smythe 8.10.1955.
19 On the right bank of the Sittang River, 125 miles north of Pegu (now Bago).
20 Ibid., p.162.
21 Ibid., p. 190.

Unknown to 1 BURDIV, the Japanese were encircling Toungoo whilst they were entraining for Taungdwingyi, near Magway; the Japanese arrived within a day of their departure. The next month was spent retreating north, digging into a position and then retreating again. What little remained of the RAF after the Japanese bombing of Magwe aerodrome, had flown from Burma leaving a morale-deficit on the ground. Unhindered, the Japanese air force bombed and burned towns across Southern and Central Burma and the Japanese-supporting Burmese also used fire as a warning of the presence of British troops, whilst gangs of Burmese *dacoits* roamed the country.

Mandalay was flattened by bombing on 3 April – hardly a Good Friday – and Maymyo followed on 6 April to add to Cecil's worries about Minny and the children. 1 BURDIV retreated to defend Yenangyaung, the heart of the oilfields of Burma; an ocean of oil derricks next to a recently evacuated prosperous town. The battle for Yenangyaung took place over a twenty square mile area bordered by the Irrawaddy to the west and the Raungdwingyi-Magwe-Yenangyaung road to the east. Between 12 and 19 April, the division fought to keep control of the oilfields that the Japanese needed so badly. By the 15 April, outflanked and struggling, the order was given to destroy the oilfields and this was done filling the skies with a pall of black smoke; millions of gallons of oil destroyed. Shattered, dehydrated soldiers of 1 BURDIV were being attacked from all directions but the cavalry were on their way in the form of the Sixty-sixth Chinese Army[22] and 38th Division. This dramatic increase in manpower allowed the exhausted division to escape over the Pin *Chaung* (watercourse). The soft sand of the *chaung* meant many of the vehicles, including full ambulances, were left behind and when a gunnery officer bravely returned that evening to rescue the wounded, he found all of them executed; bayonetted or with their throats slit. 'That our situation should have fallen to such a level that we had to abandon our wounded to the attentions of an enemy notorious for his savagery and brutality, must mark that last day of the Yenangyaung battle, 19 April 1942, as one of the blackest in the long history of British arms'.[23]

There was now only a month until the start of the monsoon which would transform the whole of Burma and make travel virtually impossible, so the retreat to India was on a tight time frame. It was agreed that the retreat would

22 Division Commander General Sun Li-jen (1900-90).
23 Carmichael, Pat, *Mountain Battery* (Bournemouth: Devin Books, 1983), p. 168.

be through Shwebo and Kalewa whose tracks through the jungle were still clogged with the thousands of refugees heading in the same direction. All travel was at night to avoid attacks from above as well as the intense heat, supplies were low but they were able to purchase food from villagers with the assistance of officers like Cecil who were fluent in Burmese.

The Japanese were close behind, often as little as one day. General Sakurai and his 33rd Division entered Pakokku less than twenty-four hours after Bourke had marched out. Pat Carmichael of 23 Mountain Battery wrote 'Night marching in these conditions was a game of follow my leader. Each man had to stick to the one in front at all costs throughout the column, and God help anyone who lost touch, for it was easy for men to do so and wander off, and in floundering about put an operation at risk.'[24] They were exhausted, hungry, thirsty, often suffering from dysentery and malaria and constantly on their guard for the enemy attack that could come at any time.

The attack came on 1 May when the Japanese crossed the River Chindwin at Monywa, occupied the town and dug-in enabling them to repel the counter-attack the next day. The Japanese set off in pursuit of the retreating Allies but by 4 May most had reached Ye-U. The obstacle of the River Chindwin was still ahead of them and the concern was of the Japanese cutting them off there, but the majority crossed the river at Shwegyin to Kalewa with the cover of air support and a Royal Marines' contingent and their guns two miles south of the crossing.

Still ahead of them was some of the toughest terrain in the world. Passable jungle tracks would become quagmires in the wet with the added worries of malaria, cholera, typhus, blackwater fever and jaundice together with ticks and leeches. There were wounded to be transported across this terrain and all around them were the thousands of struggling refugees. Lunt writes 'Refugees were everywhere, some giving birth, some dying, all utterly exhausted and without hope. Over all hung the stench of human excrement, decomposing bodies, burning trucks and tanks'.[25] 'Pat Carmichael wrote about the soldiers and their mules 'Like the animals, men and officers had lost condition badly. Men were under-weight with cheeks and eye-sockets hollowing out. Some of the *jarwans* [lads in Urdu] also had jungle sores and dysentery. But our main

24 Ibid., p. 188.
25 Lunt, James, *op. cit.*, p.256.

concern was for the *khattchars* [mules] who ... would have to do the long stretch to Shwegyin under full loads'[26]

Soldiers and refugees alike were loaded, under fire, onto steamers to cross the river and when the terrified boat crews would no longer sail, escape was on jungle tracks up to Kaing to cross opposite Kalewa. A massive British bombardment used up all the ammunition that would otherwise be abandoned and covering fire from the Bofors guns of 3 Indian LAA (Light Anti-Aircraft) Battery assisted the break out. All the big guns and most of the trucks and tanks were left behind with the exception of one tank which made it across the Chindwin and drove all the way to Imphal. *The Curse of Scotland* changed hands and fought its way back to Rangoon in 1945 as the commanding officer's tank of the 7 Light Cavalry, Indian Armoured Corps.

Cecil, meanwhile, was with 2 Burma Brigade protecting the side flanks of BURCORPS. They left Pakokku on 29 April and at Pauk he met a group of *Thakins* (Burmese Independence Army fighters). 'Merton, carrying out his duties as Brigade Intelligence Officer, was lucky to get away with his life when he encountered a large body of armed Burmese some miles east of Pauk. He was alone at the time but his command of the language probably saved him.'[27] In his notes, Cecil describes 'several hundred of the BIA, all armed with rifles, Brens etc wearing bamboo topis and red and white arm bands and carrying red and white flags. Other cars there. Stopped to call officer when saw they were not our men. Had to back about mile before found place to turn but no shots fired. Evidently thought I was one of them.'[28]

The monsoon arrived on 12 May so the final days of their trek was in torrential rains which turned *chaungs* into raging rivers and jungle paths into mud slides.

After Pauk the brigade continued their march north, through the jungles and open fields and over the many *chaungs* which tested their patience and strength having to carry the contents of each bullock cart over the streams in the heat, humidity and rain. Their final major crossing was the Manipur river and they arrived to find that the bridge had been destroyed which meant they were unable to cross with the bullock carts. The carts were destroyed and 400 bullocks were slaughtered. Finally, after fighting and marching from

26 Carmichael, Pat, *op. cit.*, p.206.
27 Lunt, James, *op. cit.*, p.259.
28 Memoirs/papers of C G Merton IWM/05/11/1.

Moulmein from the end of January, they finally stumbled into India on the 24 May. On their arrival in Imphal, Cecil succumbed to the fever that he had been fighting off since 15 April. He was evacuated to Barrackpore Reinforcement Camp at the beginning of June and once recovered, went into Calcutta to try and find out news about Minny and the children.

4

Minny

"Be stoic: just do the right thing, just keep going."
Maxime Lagacé

On arrival in Calcutta, Cecil went straight to Spences Hotel to seek information about his family's whereabouts. He assumed they were in India having made plans for their evacuation by air from Myitkyina through Captain Vesey of Military Evacuations. As he climbed the steps of the hotel, he met Bertie Castens,[1] a giant of a man who was District Forest Officer of the Katha Division. He immediately asked where Minny was and was horrified to hear that she and the children had been left behind in Katha. Castens had last seen her there on 4 May.

At the fighting crept closer to Maymyo, Minny realised the time had come to follow Cecil's instructions and get out of Burma. She enquired at Captain Vesey's offices and was told to get to Mandalay as soon as possible and then onto Myitkyina for a flight to Calcutta. She rushed home to pack for herself and the children and was able to get a lift in a truck going to Mandalay and from there, a steamer to Myitkyina. This journey normally took three days but it now took nine and at every stop to collect wood to power the steamer's engine, all the adult passengers had to go and gather wood which meant she had to, most reluctantly, leave the children alone on board whilst doing so. On their journey north the news filtered through that Myitkyina had fallen to the Japanese and the boat was diverted to Katha. Minny was fortunate in knowing Castens so, carrying her suitcase, she and the children headed for

1 Major Herbert Ernest Castens, District Forest Officer, Katha Division.

his bungalow. Staying with Castens for a couple of days, they discussed their escape from Burma. He pointed out that to attempt the journey on foot would be a death sentence for the children and the best chance they had was the camp for refugees just outside the town. In charge of the camp was U Ba Chit, a trusted member of the Forest Department. Freddie Webster, Assistant Conservator of Forests in Katha, was also present and he offered to take her to the camp in a taxi. The driver of the taxi refused to take them so Webster bought the taxi for 400 rupees and drove them to the camp. There were three hundred Burmese and Indians housed in huts called *bashas* overseen by U Ba Chit who was kind and protective.

When the Japanese took Katha, they were aware that Minny was married to a British officer and would continually interrogate her about her husband's whereabouts and would question seven-year-old June to try and catch her out. After two months in the camp, Minny boldly approached the Japanese headquarters in Katha to ask permission to go home to her bungalow near Maymyo where her family were living, and surprisingly the officer granted her permission. Kind, efficient and fatherly U Ba Chit obtained the necessary travel documents and provided an escort for them of a young, trustworthy lad from the Forest Department and they repeated their journey home. This time the steamer had an Indian crew with a Japanese captain and there was no need to collect wood. She was overjoyed to find her mother, sister and brother-in-law in the bungalow and their presence in the house had protected it from the looting that had occurred in other European homes. Shortly after their arrival, the Japanese Air Force Commanding Officer of Aniskan Airport demanded the use of her house, giving her twenty-four hours to get out, expecting the family to go and camp near the airport in some abandoned huts. Through an interpreter, she pointed out that she had two small children and an aged mother who could not possibly be expected to live under the threat of the bombing raids on the airport but that some friends had offered her a small dwelling nearby. Promising that she would inform the officer if her husband returned, she stood in the middle of the road with all her belongings around her. Thanks to the kindness of Burmese villagers, one emptied the contents of his bullock cart onto the road to allow him to convey the furniture that they needed to the hut and to sell the rest in Mandalay. The money she received from the furniture sale was the seed capital for her business venture buying fruit and vegetables cheaply in Maymyo and sending it by bullock cart along the jungle tracks to Mandalay where she sold it for a profit. Minny found a young Burman who was struggling to feed his family and he took the vegetables from the market garden that was Maymyo. Then the same cart brought back rice and oil which she sold in a small shop that she had opened in her house and in this way was able to fund and feed her family for the next three years. The round trip of seventy miles, including the time disposing of the goods, buying the return load and the resting of the bullocks, took around a week. 'Trading comes instinctively to Burmese women … it is fair to say that Burmese women were responsible for ninety five percent of the retail trade of the country and what wholesale trade was carried out was almost exclusively in the hands of the women. There are known instances of Burmese women, completely unable to read or write Burmese operating rice brokerage businesses with a monthly turnover of several hundred thousand rupees a month. It was only natural therefore that she should turn to trading as a means of making a livelihood. In this she was very successful'[2] wrote Cecil in his notes. In the garden she had over two hundred chickens until they were wiped out by chicken cholera and afterwards, she kept just enough to supply the family's needs in eggs.

Her other major concern was keeping the children looking as Burmese as possible and out of sight of the Japanese. Little Fiona was really too young to understand but she hated the Japanese and would mutter under her breath 'Go away. It is because of you that my Daddy is not here' whilst hiding under the bed. Minny had shown the children where her jewellery was hidden with the proviso that they must not tell anyone where it was unless Mummy went away for a long time.

There was a Singhalese monk living in a tiny bamboo hut nearby; born to well-to-do Buddhist parents in Ceylon, he had travelled the world, become a Christian and then returned to his Buddhist faith before settling near Maymyo. He was very devout spending his days meditating and praying, apart from when he toured the local houses with his begging bowl. He was also ferociously Pro-British and would preach against the Japanese but was never reported to the Japanese for his views because he was much admired for his total devotion to his faith. He would visit Minny daily with his begging bowl and exchange war news, excitedly once the Japanese were on the back foot. She would beg him to keep his voice down knowing that she was being watched by

2 Memoirs/papers of C G Merton IWM/05/11/1.

the Japanese. He was also keeping a diary of every Japanese plane shot down and damaged trains; the RAF were able to use this after the war to confirm 'kills'.

Minny was constantly listening out for information on the grapevine about British advances and collected propaganda leaflets to find out what was happening in the war. She always needed permission to go any distance away from her house, knowing her house was being watched all the time; she would hear dogs barking late at night and concluded that this was because of her observers.

Just as Minny was praying for liberation at the end of the war with fighting taking place around Mandalay, the Japanese moved their army HQ from Maymyo to Taunggyi and with no pack animals available to transport their equipment, decided to use all the internees to boost their coolie numbers. An English-speaking Japanese NCO arrived at the hut to tell Minny that the *Kempeitai*[3] would be coming to collect her and the children during the night, take them to Maymyo and from there they would be used as porters carrying loads over the hills to Taunggyi. She pleaded that the children were far too young and the journey of over one hundred miles on steep hill tracks in the heat would kill them but it was all in vain. She was in despair after all they had been through; she would never see Cecil again just as the end of the war was in sight. Without telling the children what awaited them, the family concluded their evening meal with a prayer meeting before putting the children to bed for one last time. At three in the morning, they heard heavy mortar fire coming from the direction of Maymyo and the threatened *Kempeitai* transport did not turn up then or later. Good news travelled fast and they heard that the British forces had arrived in Maymyo and had ambushed a convoy of lorries on the road out of the town. There was no doubt that this convoy was the one coming to pick up Minny and the others under threat. Her prayers had been answered.

A Burmese friend who was a retired senior Government official, told her that two Civil Affairs Officers had set up an office in Maymyo where enquiries could be made about missing relatives. Minny visited immediately and realised that one of the officers knew Cecil. He reassured her that Cecil was very much alive and well and advised her to write him a letter that would be passed to him. It never did make it to Cecil's hands.

3 Military Police arm of the Imperial Japanese Army.

5

Z Force

> "I remember thinking to myself as I shook hands with some of them – you are very much braver men than I can ever hope to be."
>
> Field Marshal Viscount Slim on the men of Z Force

'There is, however, one kind of special unit which should be retained – that designed to be employed in small parties, usually behind the enemy, on tasks beyond the normal scope of warfare in the field ... They will be troops, though they will require many qualities and skills not to be expected of the ordinary soldier and they will use many methods beyond his capacity ... They should rarely work within our own lines. Not costly in manpower, they may, if handled with imaginative ruthlessness, achieve strategic results'[1] wrote Field Marshall Slim in his afterthoughts chapter in *Defeat into Victory*. The lack of intelligence had concerned Slim from the moment he arrived in India. 'We were like a blind boxer trying to strike an unseen opponent and to parry blows we did not know were coming until they hit us. It was a nasty feeling.'[2]

General Headquarters Delhi housed the Military Intelligence offices and under this umbrella organisation were four sections of General Staff (Intelligence) (GS (I)). GS I (a) was Operational Intelligence, GS I (b) was Security, GS I (c) covered Censorship and Press, and GS I (x) was Intelligence Administration. During the war, this expanded with GS I (d) which was Deception, GS I (e) which covered Interrogation, GS I (s) Signal Security

1 Slim, Field Marshall Viscount, *Defeat into Victory* (London: Cassell & Company, 1956), p.627.
2 Ibid., p.35.

Lieutenant Colonel C E C Gregory. (Lieutenant General Sir Geoffrey Evans)

which was to be made part of Signals Branch and finally GS I (z) which oversaw Z Force.

Bombay, Karachi and Calcutta had offices headed by Military Intelligence Officers and Major Eric Gregory[3] was the head of Military Intelligence in Calcutta. He worked out of a Calcutta flat and oversaw defensive intelligence in India and Burma including counter-espionage and anti-sabotage. He and his team realised that Z Force could not be created using soldiers with no knowledge of the land and its people. What was needed was volunteers who spoke the language, had an affinity with its people, understood the land, could negotiate the jungle without maps and had contacts throughout the country as well as being fit, brave, loyal, independent and used to the hard life of living in the jungle. What better than the Teak Wallahs and oil company representatives

3 Lieutenant Colonel C E C Gregory OBE, The Royal Garwhal Rifles.

Lieutenant Colonel J P Shelley.
(Lieutenant General Sir Geoffrey Evans)

who had just walked out of Burma under the most horrendous of circumstances?

Lieutenant Colonel Jack Shelley[4] arrived in Delhi in early 1942 to run GS I (z) and he consulted the Burma Civil List to find suitable candidates and each choice was approached and then invited to Delhi to meet Shelley and his Personal Assistant, Pamela Caunter. His interview of the candidates would finish with asking if each had a friend that they would be willing to work and live with under the most demanding of circumstances.

Acting on Shelley's orders, Gregory began his inquiries which led him to Bertie Castens, the former District Forest Officer from Katha. This giant of a man had only recently arrived in Calcutta and was stuck in the hotel waiting for his new shoes to be made as his previous pair had not survived the walk out of Burma. He immediately agreed to join Z Force. When Cecil arrived in Calcutta and met Castens on the steps of Spences Hotel, Major J K Parry[5] was also there and together they informed Cecil that they had both been approached by Gregory and were shortly to visit Shelley in Delhi. 'Told them I was very keen to join

4 Lieutenant Colonel John Patrick Shelley (1888-1966), Royal Lancaster Regiment, Royal Flying Corps, Grenadier Guards. He had served in WWI in the Royal Flying Corps. Intelligence Officer in Sudan, Egypt and China. Seconded to the Foreign Office in Palestine. In 1939 he joined General Carton de Wiart's Mission in Poland and married a young Polish girl Sophie, who was killed after six months of marriage by Luftwaffe bombs on the village of Lukow where the mission had evacuated to.

5 Major J K Parry, Bromsgrove School, Sandhurst, previously Indian Army and subsequently Foucar Brothers and had been Cecil's Manager.

Major J K Parry MC. (Lieutenant General Sir Geoffrey Evans)

Lieutenant Colonel G W Parker DSO. (Lieutenant General Sir Geoffrey Evans)

them and they promised to put my name up'[6] wrote Cecil in his notes, planning his revenge on the Japanese for what he presumed they had done to his family.

Also approached were Denis Rae,[7] Sam Newland[8] and Freddie Webster[9] who, like Castens, worked for the Burma Forest Service and Robin Stewart,[10] Dickie Wood,[11] Jimmy Middleton[12] and George Parker[13] who worked for the

6 Memoirs/papers of C G Merton IWM/05/11/1.
7 Captain Denis Wilmot Rae, born in Burma to Anglo-Indian parents. Attended Maymyo boarding school.
8 Major S Newland DSO, born in Fort Haka in 1900, son of an Indian Medical Service Major and his Chin wife. Attended Maymyo School with Rae.
9 Major F V Webster MC, born to Anglo-Indian parents in India.
10 Major J R Stewart MC, Fettes and Cambridge educated before he joined the Bombay Burma Trading Corporation.
11 Major R W Wood MC, educated at Wellington and Cambridge, he became a Forest Assistant in 1937 and was commissioned into the Burma Rifles in 1940.
12 Major J G Middleton, son of Anglo-Burman parents, excellent shot and well-known big game hunter, official of the Bombay Burma Trading Corporation.
13 Lieutenant Colonel G W Parker DSO, MBE, MC, Cambridge educated, nicknamed 'Red'. Forest Manager of the Bombay Burma Trading Corporation, walked out of Burma with his wife and bull terriers.

Bombay Burma Trading Corporation. A decision that needed to be made was what to call these ten volunteers and it was agreed to call them the British Officer Johnnies or BOJs, a name that could be used in conversation or on a radio message without giving away their secret purpose. 'It was then that we got the name of B.O.J.'s Z, among other activities which I never fathomed but I know extended into the Near East and the North West Frontier, was responsible for the post Occupational Intelligence in case India was invaded and overrun. For this 'agents' were secretly trained in the use of the same sets as we were given and disguised technicians in the dead of night who would install these in most improbable places. These were a constant source of trouble to our technicians as, owing to the nature of the places where they had to be hidden, damp was always getting in or rats would gnaw the connections. These agents were always known by the code name of 'Johnnies' and we, being British Officers were known as B O Johnnies'.[14]

Shelley's liaison officer was Major Arthur Goring[15] and his assistant was Major A Shuttleworth[16] and from their office in Calcutta, they were to give the Johnnies' patrols all the latest information before they set off and to interrogate them on their return.

One of the most important aspects of their job was communication and the conventional army wireless sets were far too heavy and with too limited a range for the distances concerned. A workshop was set up in Delhi and two members of Burma Oil's wireless and telephone service team, R C Jones and A T A Mendes together with Majors Hills and Jones, worked tirelessly gathering parts from bazaars across India. They created a set that weighed twenty-five pounds, operated telephonically and was recharged with a hand powered car dynamo which weighed another thirty pounds. One hour's winding produced ten minutes' talking time. 'They produced a hand dynamo using a car dynamo with handle. This never proved satisfactory as they could only get brass gears which expanded after much turning and became very stiff. Wretched men were put on to turning this handle in relays for about 12 hours at a time'[17]

14 Memoirs/papers of C G Merton IWM/05/11/1.
15 Major A A Goring, Probyn's Horse, Intelligence Directorate in Hong Kong until the invasion, liason officer with Eastern Army Headquarters.
16 Major Anthony T St J Shuttleworth OBE.
17 Memoirs/papers of C G Merton IWM/05/11/1.

Major F V Webster MC. (Lieutenant General Sir Geoffrey Evans)

Major J R Stewart MC. (Lieutenant General Sir Geoffrey Evans)

Major R W Wood MC. (Lieutenant General Sir Geoffrey Evans)

Major S Newland DSO. (Lieutenant General Sir Geoffrey Evans)

Major C G Merton MC and bar. (Family Archives)

wrote Cecil. Each year an improved model was brought out until they finished the war on Mark IV.

Receiving stations in Calcutta, Shillong, Imphal and Delhi were manned by four or five women per detachment on six or eight hours' watch, listening continuously. They sweated in the heat, day and night, wrapped up against the mosquitoes, receiving high praise from the men in the jungle. Occasionally the machines broke down; once when a lizard crawled into the condenser. A code was chosen which was never broken by the Japanese and the women operators learnt each of the individual Johnnie's voices as well as a secondary numerical code to use should they be put under duress by the enemy. A personal piece of information was used to prove the identity of each man such as the name of his Great Aunt's dog. Cecil wrote 'There were some very charming WAAC(I)s doing the signals. They were also being trained at the same time and later were greatly expanded and did most sterling work under most discouraging conditions. They always took an immense interest in each party and were very good to us when we returned from patrols.'[18]

At the beginning of July all the Johnnie's went to Delhi to see Shelley and Brigadier Cawthorne[19] and preparations and plans were made. There were a series of interviews with the heads of various departments; Ordnance, Supplies and Medical. Ordnance produced light weight tents and light rifles. The Medical Department decided on which rations provided the necessary calorific content and the lightest weight for carrying. Each party carried three large

18 Ibid.

19 Major General Sir Walter J Cawthorne CB, CIE, CBE (1896-1970), Australian Imperial Force, 46th Punjabis, 16th Punjabis, Middle East Intelligence, GS I (d).

medical panniers full of drugs such as Sulphanilamide, an anti-bacterial drug used throughout the war to combat infection and Mepacrine for malaria.

More recruits were added eventually to the original ten; Robin Stewart brought Willy Goldberg[20] on board, Dicky Wood brought in Tim Dix.[21] They all knew what a terrible fate was in store for them if they were captured by the Japanese and that there was no help to be had from the outside if under attack or struck down by illnesses.

The patrol areas were agreed: Number One party was Castens and Webster and would cover the Mansi Forest between Homalin and Tonhe on the Chindwin reaching east to Katha. Number Two party was Stewart and Wood on either side of the Chindwin from Tonhe to Yuwa. Number Three party was Parker and Middleton in the Kabaw and Kale valleys and down the Chindwin from Mawlaik to Paluzawa. Number Four party was Newland and Rae in the Chin Hills and the Gangaw Valley and Number Five party was Parry and Merton to go south of the Chin Hills to the Mon valley.

Each party was to consist of two officers and a minimum of eight men, each carrying a rucksack weighing forty-five pounds when full and a cut down rifle, latterly a Sten gun. Two wireless sets were carried per party in case of breakdowns, a shotgun to shoot game for the pot and the medical bags with quinine, sulpha and bandages. Sealed tins held tea, powdered milk, salt, Marmite, biscuits, curry powder, rice, salt ghee, potatoes, dried onions and dhal and treats such as bacon, jam, butter and bully beef. Saccharine instead of sugar and some foul-smelling Vitamin sweets which made everything else smell. 'One could disguise the taste in the food but not in the tea and I will never forget that horrible concoction we used to drink – add powdered milk in a kerosene tin with the top two or three inches removed. Each tin was one day's ration for the party. The total was to be buried. The total weight was about 28lbs and it was air proof so that they could be carried on the back by our men or Chin coolies who carry their loads on their backs, or one at each end of a pole to be carried by Burmese coolies who carry in this manner.'[22] Food supplies would be buried in hidden dumps so that they did not need to be carried. Despite all the attempts at having as balanced a diet as was possible

20 Major William Archibald Goldberg, Indian Intelligence Corps.
21 Second Lieutenant T Dix, Royal Corps of Signals.
22 Memoirs/papers of C G Merton IWM/05/11/1.

under the circumstances, by the time they returned to India from each operation, they were suffering from incipient scabies and their teeth were becoming loose in their gums.

Cecil and Parry decided to go 'down to our old Mon Chaung area through Chin Hills and get information in that area. Such was ignorance of true situation in G.H.Q. that told to feel our way cautiously as far as Lungleh and try to get agents out from there.'[23] Shelley fully understood that these men knew their areas better than he did and that they should make the bulk of the decisions.

Early on in his time in Delhi, Cecil was approached by an Indian fortune teller, 'I am not normally a great believer in such people but he had some very strong letters of recommendation from important personages and being so anxious about my wife and children I was glad to try anything that might rightly or wrongly give me some reason for optimism. I must admit what he told me impressed me. He had no means of obtaining any information about me as is the practise of many of these sages. I had no servants with me and I was a stranger only just arrived in a strange hotel. He told me that I was very worried about my wife and that she was equally worried about me but that we were prevented from communicating with one another as though an impassable wall separated us and we were each trying to find a means of getting through this wall. He assured me that in spite of everything there was no need to worry, that they were safe and no harm would come to them. I was quite content to pay the 50R which was his fee and he must have been surprised that I did question him further as to my future prospects and seek advice as to my career which, from the testimonials he carried, he was an expert at doing. He told me that we would eventually come together again and then spend a long and happy life together without further separations. I can only hope that this will prove correct.'[24]

Whilst still in Delhi, Cecil heard that All India Radio was broadcasting messages from refugees to family and friends still in Burma. He found the Director very sympathetic and he put Cecil in touch with Dora Tan Aye who was a well-known Rangoon broadcaster in charge of the Burma broadcasts. He wrote a message in both English and Burmese and she promised that it would be broadcast on three consecutive days. Wary of putting his family in

23 Ibid.
24 Ibid.

more danger, he sent a message that would only be understood by Minny or close friends, using nicknames. It read: 'To Minny from Micky. Am safe and well and hope you, June and Fiona are the same. Do not despair. Am thinking of you always. Will any friends who receive this message please pass it on … I am happy to say that this message was received some six months later by my wife and relieved her immensely as up to that time she had no idea what had become of me since I left her on 1st April 1942 and was constantly speculating as to whether I had been killed or captured on the way out. Being worried about this she made enquiries from any person who had returned from Myitkyina etc when they found they could not get to India or persons who had been arrested by the Japs and subsequently released. Contacting such people was dangerous and they were never free from suspicion and anyone seen to be seeking them out also came under suspicion. The Jap suspicion of 'Spies' amounted to almost a mania. After every heavy air [raid] people were rounded up and accused of signalling to our aircraft. The fact that they had no means of signalling meant nothing to the Japs, they said they had put out their laundry to dry in a special manner or shown lights. They were constantly making surprise raids in the hope of finding a transmitter and a piece of wire found in your compound was enough to have you arrested as possessing a wireless with which you were in communication with the enemy. Wireless receiver sets were all confiscated under the excuse that they wanted to cut out the frequencies that we were broadcasting on from India but there were very few people who received them back again after this operation. The majority were sent to Rangoon and shipped to Japan, for converting to military sets. People were arrested for possessing hair pins or smelling of carbolic soap as they said that they were not available in Burma and so must have been dropped in payment for information supplied.'[25]

He also had a close shave before the Johnnies set off for Calcutta. He dined with his friend Frank Reynolds, previously Deputy Superintendent of Police in Katha, who said he was intending to parachute into Katha and would Cecil join him. So great was his desire to find Minny and the children who were last seen in U Ba Chit's camp in Katha, that he considered it to get his family out but 'I told him I would be delighted to join him but could not let Parry and Z down and somebody else would have to be found to partner Parry … I gave

25 Ibid.

him my address in Calcutta at Spences Hotel where we intended to stay for 10 days collecting the last articles of our equipment. He said he would see his boss next day and I could rest assured that I would be accompanying him on his mission and he would see me in Calcutta where he was due in 5 days' time. This was the last time I ever saw Frank; he jumped into Katha near Wuntho and contacted one of his policemen who handed him over to the Japs the same day … There are rumours that he was tortured and then shot in Rangoon but I have never been able to substantiate this.'[26]

At the end of July, the Johnnies were almost ready to set off from Delhi to Calcutta but several delays held them up due to the hospitalisation of one of the men and the wireless sets needing more work on them. During this period, they got permission to take their men to Alipore and Dum Dum Air Fields to show them the might of the RAF as up until that point they had only seen Japanese airplanes. They were most impressed with the Hurricanes and early Spitfires but disappointed with how few aircraft there were to take on the mighty Japanese Air Force. A young Arakanese soldier, Tai Cawn[27] was concerned that these were the only aircraft and was assured that there were countless airfields across India with many more aircraft. Cecil wounded his arm during this period and for a time afterwards was plagued by boils at the site of the wound.

Finally, on 6 August they set off on the 0635 train to Chittagong and were seen off by officers from their Headquarters. A special compartment was booked for the men so that they did not come into contact with other troops and be tempted to talk about their destination. Secrecy was imperative and few knew of their existence. To keep this clandestine, Cecil was 'posted' in army orders as Captain, Intelligence Officer, G H Q Delhi and was teased by friends about the 'cushy job I had got for myself and it was hard not to be able to disillusion them'.[28] They were unable to post letters home once they left Calcutta but it was agreed that Air Graphs would be sent informing families that they were unable to write themselves but were safe and healthy. After

26 Ibid.

27 Tai Cawn (Taik Chun and Tsai Cawn are alternative spellings) from the Arakan Yomas, joined the army at 14 as a bugler boy and rose to the rank of captain in the Burmese Army. He was awarded the Aung San Thuriya, the equivalent of the V.C., (instituted in 1948 for valour and gallantry) fighting rebels in the Arakan.

28 Ibid.

the war Cecil discovered that these had not been sent to his parents causing a lot of distress and anxiety. 'They had already suffered enough during the total breakdown of mail services in the first Burma campaign when for three months they received no news of me only newspaper accounts of the relentless Japanese advance and the broadcast news at the end of April that the major portion of the Burma Army must be considered as lost. It was never expected that General Alexander would succeed in extracting almost his entire army. If I had not relied on their promise I could easily have written to my parents and warned them not to worry but for some time I would not be in a position to write to them'[29]

On arrival in Chittagong, Brigade Headquarters advised Cecil how to get to Rangamatti and a military launch was arranged for early the following morning to allow them to set off up the River Carmafouli (now called Karnaphuli). The launch was prepared for war with a Bren gun mounted on the roof and a wireless calling out 'all quiet' at intervals but the body of the launch was filled with bales of hay, surprisingly.

They arrived at Rangamatti after dark in continuous rain and Colonel Hyde, the Deputy Commissioner Chittagong, was waiting for them with a meal and accommodation for the men and an invitation for dinner and a night's stay for Cecil. Cecil joined him for dinner but preferred to stay with his men in the Circuit House.

Deciding to test the men and their equipment, a trial patrol was run out of Rangamatti with a local policeman as a guide and all their packs full to bursting with everything they would be carrying for real. The trial run also sorted out some unsuitable men, a couple of Lushais,[30] 'The missionaries may have converted the Lushais into Christians but they have also converted them into a spineless, effeminate crowd, no use for our purpose.'[31] They were useful at first as interpreters as they knew the local languages which helped as the policeman/guide they had been given turned out to be a complete stranger to the area as well as a new recruit to the police. The conditions on the six-day muddy march were appalling but it tested them for what was to come and

29 Ibid.

30 Lushais (Cecil's spelling), Lushei or Lushay, one of the 53 ethnic sub-groups that make up the Chin tribe.

31 Ibid.

was, in Cecil's words, 'Interesting and instructive.'[32] The rations were proved satisfactory although more salt and less curry powder was needed. Salt, rubber boots and ammunition were requested by wire to Parry who was to join them shortly.

On their return to Rangamatti, Cecil went down with a bout of malaria as well as extreme rheumatic pain and a septic thumb. A doctor at the hospital declared it was a 'waitlow' that needed lancing and as Cecil walked to the bed where the procedure was to take place, six men came in too and Cecil took them to be medical students. With a shortage of Novocaine, they were actually there to hold the patient down but with 'supreme control I rendered the six men superfluous.'[33]

After spending three weeks in Rangamatti waiting for the arrival of Parry, Cecil decided to take his men to Lungleh in the Southern Lushai Hills to regain his health. They travelled by launch up the river to Barkal and then onto Demagiri before a three day march up to the hill town of Lungleh. It was home to one of the men and Cecil watched a touching reunion with his parents who thought he was killed in Burma. After a few days rest and another test patrol, they set out on the final leg of their long-awaited return to Burma. Crossing the Boinu River balancing on a wire rope followed by four days marching, they entered Thingsai which was the ultimate village before the border. The village hosted a party in their honour, drinking tea and singing hymns and making welcome speeches to which Cecil was expected to reply. He made fifteen speeches and finished the evening singing *One man went to mow* and *Clementine* whilst the four Karen soldiers in his party responded with their renditions of Karen songs. At the time they thought it was a jolly party until they went to the non-Christian Chin parties over the border where their parties consisted of 'drinking, dancing, drinking, singing, drinking, feasting, drinking and more drinking and the drinks are not of the soft variety.'[34]

The River Tyao forms the boundary between the Indian Lushai Hills and the Burmese Chin Hills. The Indian village Thingsai was situated at 4500 feet and they descended to the river at 1400 feet and then up again to Bunkhua at 5500 feet. Another wire rope bridge had been rigged up to cross the river with a small wooden cage to carry people and equipment and winched across by the

32 Ibid.
33 Ibid.
34 Ibid.

Haka Barracks and civil quarters. The Japanese sheltered in the jungle beyond the village. (Lieutenant General Sir Geoffrey Evans)

Chins on the other side of the river. There was great rejoicing from the men, especially the Chins, to be back in Burma at last. Cecil was soon to be on the receiving end of Chin hospitality.

On entering the villages of Phungkah, Thangzang and Sinhmuh, passing the flat, carved stones that protect the burial mounds of long-dead chiefs, they were met by the village Chief wearing his best silk blanket accompanied by all the village elders. The Chief greeted Cecil with a mug of *Zu Rau*, the local beer brewed from rice which he found refreshing at first but as they marched on in the heat to the next village and the next offering of beer, he found himself marching in a haze to the final village and the many more pots of beer that were waiting for them. Each village has Rest Houses made of either bamboo or pine planks topped with thatched roofs and this was where they were to sleep before two more days of marching to their destination of Haka.

On their arrival on 3 October in Haka they were greeted by Joshua Poo Nye, the Assistant Superintendent, who was in a similar position as Cecil worrying about his wife and family who were in the Delta when Burma fell and he was unaware of their fate. He was visited by Captain David James,[35] previously a Forest Assistant with the Bombay Burma Trading Company, and now with the Western Chin Levies. Poo Nye and Colonel Haswell,[36] the Officer Commanding Chin Hills Levies in Falam offered Cecil every assistance and persuaded him not to move south through the Hills to Minbu District as there was strong anti-British feeling there. An ex-Burma Rifle *Subedar* (Burmese officer) Van Tu Maing, who had been dishonourably discharged from the army, was very anti-British and pro-Japanese and had raised a force of Chin Boks and was threatening to march on Haka. Cecil started making enquiries into operating in the Gangaw Valley instead whilst waiting for the arrival of Parry with the wireless set. Parry arrived with the precious set on 14 October having nursed it diligently; he did not even unpack it for fear of damaging it. The wireless was needed the very next day when they heard the news that the Japanese had advanced up the track towards Zokhua and had engaged with the Western Chin Levies led by James, who had inflicted 50 casualties but the advance was continuing. Cecil and Parry put together their first message only to find that the prized wireless set did not work and they were back to square one with communication.

Unable to work as Intelligence gatherers in this area, they volunteered to stay in the area and make themselves useful as Levy Officers which made them most unpopular in Delhi who thought they should have returned immediately. Reinforcements were asked for from Falam and Major T T West[37] arrived on 17 October with a disciplined but untested force of Frontier Force Rifles. He was fearless and much beloved by the Chins and could drink any of them under the table; an ability which was much admired by them all. Chin men, women and children drank heavily but appeared unharmed by their excess being a strong, virile race. It was thought that the yeast in the fermentation process provided supplements that they were otherwise missing. The missionaries, who had retreated to India leaving their bungalow empty, may have been appalled by the parties that were held in their home, now inhabited by the Johnnies.

It was reported that the Japanese were closing in on Haka so it was decided to fight a delaying action and then fall back where the 600 strong Levy and Frontier Force units were based. Cecil, Parry and their party of ten men went

35 Captain David Thomas James MC, Western Chin Hills Levies.
36 Lieutenant Colonel Francis William Haswell DSO, Burma Frontier Force.
37 Major T T West, Chin Hills Battalion.

Haka women at a secret refugee camp near Haka. (Lieutenant General Sir Geoffrey Evans)

out to hold the track by the suspension bridge over the River Boimu, with orders to destroy the bridge if the Japanese threatened it.

In the meantime, their house in Haka was unguarded and, on their return, they found that all their equipment and stores were gone. Expecting Haka to fall, the Chins were determined to leave nothing for the Japanese. Anything of value that could not be carried was hidden in the jungle and all the pigs and fowl were slaughtered resulting in several continuous nights of feasting, and of course, drinking. And with drinking went the letting off of guns. The Chins were remarkable shots and prized marksmanship very highly. The sounds of boisterous explosions could be heard echoing around the hills making it difficult to ascertain which direction they were coming from, the Johnnies presumed that Haka had fallen and hurriedly hid more of the stores including two boxes with over 2,000R in silver coins; it was not where they left it on their return and three un-trustworthy members of the party were let go.

On the morning of 18 October, the party took up their defensive positions approaching the suspension bridge overlooking a bucolic, meandering river; idyllic by day but unpleasantly cold by night. At over 4600 feet above sea level and during the cold season, they froze and were unable to light fires. In desperation, Parry and Cecil moved into the same tent to share blankets, as did all the men, and the extra tent was used as an over-blanket. Rain, cold and very small tents with two men in each meant little sleep but that trip was only six days. Each day either Cecil or Parry would walk the sixteen miles to Haka and back to report and learn about the latest situation. The Japanese did not continue their advance on Zokhua, buried their dead and then withdrew to Kanpetlet which was known to be the Headquarters of Van Thu Maung.

It was then decided that Cecil would command a party of Frontier Force Rifles with 50 Levies, armed with a two-inch mortar, to hold a position near Sumsi village near the Headquarters of Van Thu Maung, the leader of the Chin Boks. A four-day 40-mile march followed, led by Cecil alongside an old *Subedar* who was previously the Senior Governor's Commission Officer in the Chin Hills. Immaculately turned out, he fostered Cecil's determination to always be aware of his appearance and to shave every day however little water was available.

At each overnight stop a small camp was built. Each had their allotted tasks. The mule drivers would feed and water their animals whilst the fire-wood detail went out to collect what was needed including grasses and saplings. Two small huts were built for Parry and Cecil and a larger one for the men. Each had thatched walls and roof with a grass covered platform forming a bed. Within two hours of halting, the camp was completed and Cecil would be sitting on his 'bed' drinking tea. With full rations and a dry hut to sleep in, Cecil felt the best he had since leaving India.

With their camp built overlooking the river, patrols were sent out daily looking for the enemy, a warning system was set up between the Johnnies and friendly local villagers and withdrawal routes were planned. No attack came and Parry and Cecil agreed that it was time to get another wireless set and return to their planned roles as intelligence gatherers. In the meantime, another Z Force party had arrived in Haka, commanded by Newlands and Rae and planning to cover the area to the East. Sammy Newlands was the son of a British Army Medical Officer and his mother was the sister of a Haka chief; he was highly respected by the Chins. An outstanding shot, fluent in the language and so admired that even his personal sobriety was forgiven. 'He recruited his band of followers locally and it was certain that every one of them would far rather be killed defending him than return to his village and report that 'Sunny Boi Pa' had been killed while he was there. He was known all over the hills as 'Sunny Boi Pa'. Sunny being his father's name for him and Boi Pa, the suffix attached to all Europeans like 'Smith Sahib' in India or 'Tuan Jones' in Malaya'.[38]

Newlands and Rae found that their wireless was not working either so it was agreed that Newlands and Parry would stay in the Chin Hills establishing contacts and Rae and Cecil would return to India to sort out the sets and each took two men from their respective parties. Their route was North West instead of the Western route used on the outward journey and by doing a double march daily, they expected to make Calcutta by Christmas. Falam informed them that there was a downed American pilot who needed to get back to India too and he was to join them for the journey. His plane had been crippled and unable to climb over the Chin Hills, he had bailed out before crashing and had landed in a plantain tree. The Levies had brought him to Falam and he was expecting to walk alone out of Burma so was much relieved to do so with these knowledgeable old hands. They pooled their rations and ate well, walked fast and were entertained royally in villages in Burma and over the Indian border into the Lushais Hills. From the town of Aijal where there was a Brigade Headquarters, a truck was made available for them to the village of Sairang where they could get a boat down the River Dhaleswari to the rail-head at Lalaghat. The boat journey was so dull and boring that Cecil started calculating how far he had walked since leaving Chittagong in August. He reckoned that it was 933 miles of hill country little realising that the following year he would walk another 2247 miles between February and Christmas 1943.

They arrived in Lalghat in the small hours of Christmas Eve delighted with the knowledge that they would make Calcutta in time for Christmas and were day-dreaming about the food and entertainment awaiting them, but the train drew to a grinding halt just before Barrackpore and they watched the search lights over Calcutta as the Japanese launched an air raid over the city. Chaos ruled and it took two hours to get a taxi to the Grand Hotel where there were no rooms or dinner to be had. As a result, the Christmas that they were so looking forward to was spent sleeping on the floor of the Grand Hotel's lounge with their usual rations for Christmas Dinner.

38 Ibid.

A warm welcome was waiting for them from Colonel Gregory and he sent off a wire to Delhi to announce their arrival and by return there was a wire requesting their immediate departure to Delhi. Cecil wrote his report of the situation in the Chin Hills on Boxing Day before departing for Delhi. He praised the Zokhua Levies but not the Sakta and Khuapi Levies or the Burma Rifles. From an Intelligence point of view, he considered that the Japanese had no idea what Allied forces were in the Chin Hills but were trying to get their own agents into the area. The Japanese were offering a reward of 1,000R for any captured British Officer handed over to them and then widened the offer to include Chins, telling the Burmans to arrest any Chins who came down from the hills.

Seats were booked for that night's train but their filthy clothes were ragged and with the shops shut the Colonel and his assistant lent them each a uniform, ill-fitting but clean and un-tattered, to tide them over their trip. Arrangements were made for the men to stay with the Burma Navy in Calcutta in Cecil and Rae's absence.

In Delhi there were rooms for them in Maidens Hotel and a fine welcome was waiting for them from Colonel Shelley and his staff. There were rounds of meetings with all the top brass and their failure to return as soon as their lack of communication was discovered appeared to have been forgiven. During Cecil's long marches in the Chin Hills, he had thought up a scheme which Shelley showed interest in called The New Burma Movement. This was then passed on to Major General Cawthorne, the Director of Military Intelligence who interviewed Cecil about it along with a request to visit the Burma Government in exile in Simla.

Having failed to celebrate Christmas at all, they were able to do New Year's Eve in style and joined Colonel Shelley's party at Maidens Hotel for a lavish dinner with plenty of champagne followed by an after party in the bungalow belonging to a Director of the hotel, where they partied into the night on French liqueurs. A slight change from *Zu* beer in *bashas* in the middle of the Chin Hills.

On 5 January Cecil set off for Simla to meet Mr Wallace, the Indian Civil Service Defence Secretary and the Chief Secretary. Wallace assumed that Cecil would want to run this scheme himself and was surprised when Cecil ruled himself out due to his lack of administrative experience. He then realised that they had assumed he was just after a cushy desk job and were mildly surprised that he was not. He realised that his plan showed up 'the great gulf between the idealistic enthusiasm which inspired the front line and the jealousies, suspicion and intrigue that one so often found in the rear.'[39] Nothing ever came of his scheme despite the interest that was expressed in Simla.

In discussions for their future role, they heard that a motor road was being constructed from Imphal to Tiddim in the Chin Hills. There was also a suggestion of a jeep track from Tiddim to Falam which would allow them to take a good supply of rations with them. Jeeps were still quite scarce in India but Z Force had priority and they were soon to have two issued to them. Trailers were requested as well as Sten guns which they trialled on the ranges used by the Viceroy's Bodyguard and they were most impressed by their weight, rapid fire and light ammunition.

Back in Calcutta they ordered three months of rations as they were to have the jeeps and trailers to transport them but it transpired that the springs on the trailers were not strong enough for the loads they were to carry. Re-fitted with stronger springs, there still was no room for luxuries so the tinned fruits were left behind with their very grateful landlady of the boarding house.

39 Ibid.

6

Lungngo

"Similar to hunting a wounded tiger."
Lieutenant-General Geoffrey Scoones

On the night of 3 February, they entrained with their jeeps and trailers on two railway flats, sleeping with their jeeps for fear of them going astray. They crossed the Brahmaputra by ferry from Pandu to Gauhati and drove on from there, sleeping and cooking on the roadside with a small transistor radio to listen to the news on All India Radio. The tow bar of one of the jeeps was not up to the task and it gave way causing an extra wait while it was mended and finally arrived in Imphal in the early hours of 12 February. It was there that they discovered that the Tiddim road was not nearly as advanced as they had been told and that they would not get through with the jeeps after all. After two days of trying to find labour to carry their loads it was agreed that their supplies would be dropped by air and they would continue on foot as before. A month's worth of supplies was selected and forty porters were found to help them as far as the Chin Hills; little realising that it would be ten weeks before the first air drop.

The march took them up a long zig-zagging track from the Beltong Lui River at 150 feet to Tiddim at an impressive 5,600 feet. Once the motor road was completed, it too climbed this series of hair pin bends and was known as 'The Chocolate Stairway'. An uneventful march took them to Haka, arriving on 13 March and while the men were having firing practice on the Sten guns, Cecil was consulting with the Zone Commander of the Levies, Captain Cozens. It was decided that the village of Shurkhua near Lungngo would make the best place for their Headquarters leaving their supplies and their 'Chore Horse',

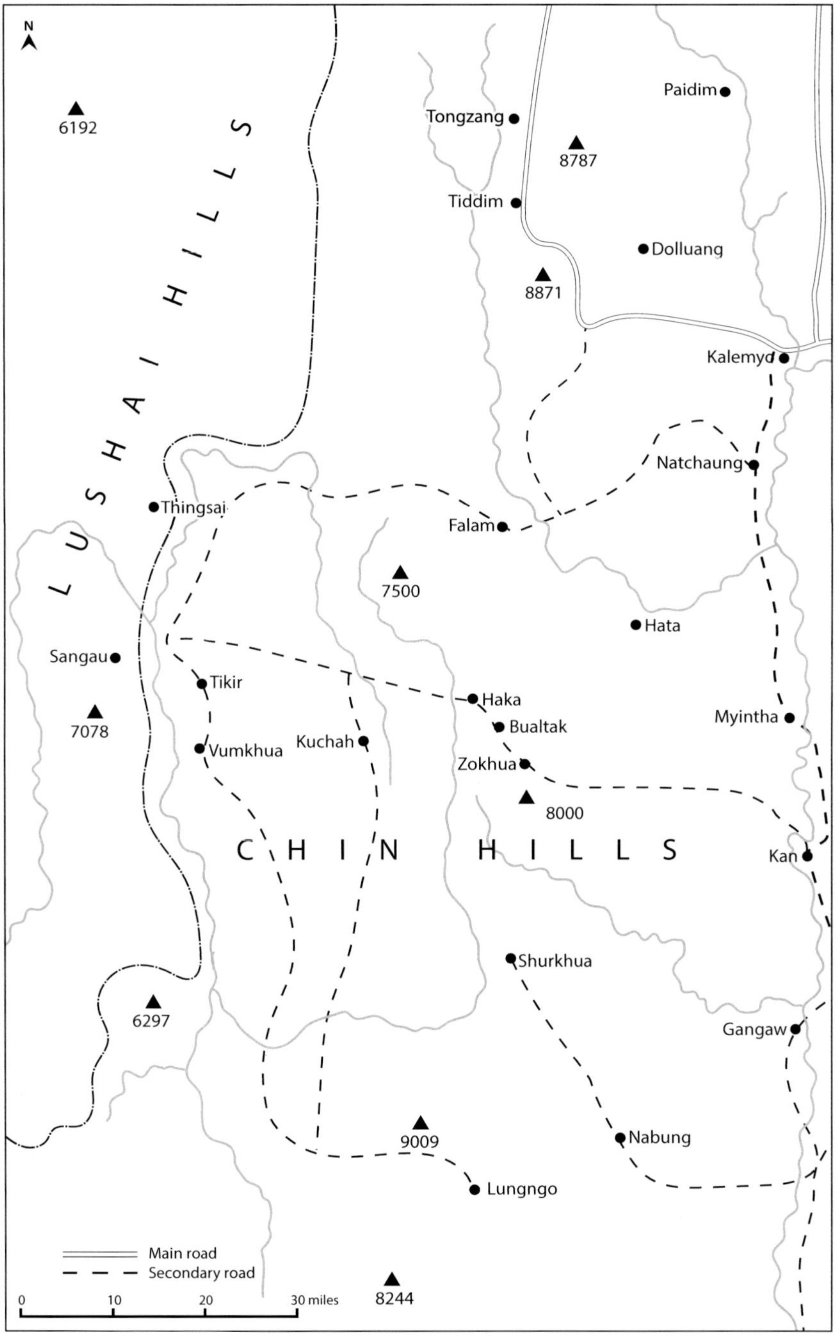

Lungngo-Shurkhua.

the petrol engine which charged the batteries. This had been carried as far as Tiddim, slung between two men but, incredibly, was carried on the back of a slender girl over the hills from Tiddim to Lungngo.

The new Assistant Superintendent of Haka was Gilbert Turnbull[1] who had walked out of Wa State on the Chinese border into India with his small force of 25 Frontier Force Rifles. His wife was Burmese and her fearless brother Thein Maung had assisted in their escape by providing intelligence about the Japanese positions. Under the auspices of Turnbull, Cecil was to attend a Chief's Meeting on 16 March to meet all the local Chiefs and Turnbull had strongly recommended Van Kio, the Chief of Shurkhua.

Their arrival in Shurkhua after a two-day march was greeted with the usual Chin hospitality and customary drinks. Chief Van Kio invited Cecil back to his house and they were to develop a strong friendship. All the men were accepted by the villagers which Cecil considered extraordinary as Chins were known to not easily accept men from the other indigenous tribes of Burma.

The village was 50 miles south of Haka, close to the plains and had the security of two Levy outposts on the trails leading to it at Dumva and Pangua which meant they would have an early warning system if the Japanese were to encroach. Their HQ was a pine bungalow which served as the village Rest House on a small hill overlooking the village. After charging their batteries and packing up some rations, a patrol set off to the outpost at Dumva, armed with a letter from Van Kio to the Headman of Dumva requesting assistance and a guide. Thanks to Japanese threats, none of the villagers were prepared to act as guide down on the plains apart from the old Headman, almost blind with cataracts, and he accompanied them and even carried a load for them despite feeling it was beneath his position. Finally, the Johnnies were having their 'first real experience of functioning as a 'Z' patrol and what we have been anticipating doing for months'[2] and despite the lack of a sighted guide and some unseasonable rain they carried on to the Vapi Va River to try and identify Japanese units using the road from Pakko-Ku to Kalemyo, covering their tracks in the sand at the crossing over the river and no longer using the established jungle tracks. Climbing up a razor-back ridge running north to south at over 1,000 feet in an area called Rangfi Kuang would allow them a perfect view of

1 Gilbert Turnbull MBE, Burma Frontier Service, previously in Wa State on the Chinese border.
2 Memoirs/papers of C G Merton IWM/05/11/1.

the road to count and identify Japanese traffic. Being the dry season, there was little tree cover and open country allowing one to see for half a mile. Whilst checking the maps with a home-made torch made of a car bulb in a condensed milk can connected to a battery, Kya Twe dropped it and it clattered on the rocks, flashing its light around the treetops briefly before they could disconnect the battery. This was spotted by a picket on the river below and shortly before dawn a Japanese spotter plane known as a 'Little Willie' flew over them, searching the hillsides. This plane was to return around lunchtime and circled them for 30 minutes and later in the day they spotted three men ducking down hurriedly half a mile away. Fearing they were encircled, the Johnnies slipped away and marched for most of the night and all the next day until they arrived exhausted in Dumva. Their maps had proved to be inaccurate and all the water sources marked were picketed by the enemy and only by getting lost had they been able to slake their thirst and fill their water bottles from a small pool of rain water which had collected on some rocks.

Cecil felt that occasionally he was 'saved by Divine intervention ... On so many occasions something I had planned went wrong and I cursed my bad luck at the time but it was later to prove my salvation. Finally, I was so convinced of this that I was content to volunteer for anything, however hopeless it might appear to me at the time with the conviction that something would intervene to prevent disaster. I felt it was up to me to plan everything very carefully and take all precautions and avoid all bravado and it would work out alright in the end.'[3]

On their return they heard the news that their presence had indeed stirred the hornet's nest. 'Two columns of Japs each with two officers and about 100 men equipped with mortars and machine guns had come out doing a pincer movement round Rangfi Klang. One column had come from Minywa and gone up into the hills to Nabung village, about 12 miles south east of Dumva while the other, coming from Gangaw had made a sweep up the Sawnkyun River valley. We still, of course, knew nothing of Wingate's expedition and so were very mystified but somewhat flattered that we should have been taken so seriously by the Japs. When I returned to India and learned of Wingate's campaign it was evident that they had mistaken us for another of his columns. That would explain why no one had fired on us when we were spotted. Seeing

3 Ibid.

a British officer, they must have assumed that he had a column halted somewhere near and were following us to discover its whereabouts.'[4]

Wingate's Chindits had launched *Operation Longcloth* with approximately 3,000 men in February 1943 so their patrols were well under way at this point but with limited communication, the Johnnies were totally unaware of this development. The receiver of the wireless set was no longer working but would still transmit so Cecil set up a Heath-Robinson-contraption with the small transistor radio set to receive while he transmitted on the larger wireless.

Exhausted, they spent a week resting and during that time went on a fishing expedition accompanied by most of the village youth, climbing down the two thousand feet to the River Boinu. Disobeying all the world's game laws they unsportingly exploded grenades into the water and picked up the stunned fish for a feast that night and smoked fish for the coming weeks. Rations were almost exhausted so the smoked fish were an important nutritional addition to their diet. They also had to resort to *myauk oo* (monkey eggs) which were large starchy tubers found ten feet underground which were utterly tasteless; the villagers found and ate them only in times of famine. Whilst at their HQ there were chickens and eggs but no vegetables, whereas on the patrols, they were only eating one tin of bully beef with rice per day and restricting their milk and sugar intake to one tin per two days which gave them two cups of tea per day per person. Disappointed by the intelligence learned during this first patrol and aware that the Japanese held the upper hand, the patrol did however give them confidence in the villager's support and loyalty.

The next patrol gleaned more information when they set out on 10 March for a 44 mile, three-day march for Lungngo. *En route* they met a group of villagers from Badufi who informed them about troop movements in their thousands across Arakan to Kanpetlet. Captain David Cozens[5] was stationed in Lungngo with his platoon of Frontier Force Rifles and 50 Levies also produced good intelligence for Cecil. Informing him that villagers to the south of Lungngo believed that all the British had either been killed or left for India and that the Japanese were in complete control of Asia.

Cozens and Cecil became very good friends but they did not see each other again until 1947 when flying home on a BOAC flying boat. They got

4 Ibid.

5 Captain David Cozens MC, previously with the Burma Oil Company and now commanding a platoon of Frontier Force Rifles.

into conversation on the third day of the flight and when Cecil said he was returning to Rangoon, Cozens asked 'You don't know Micky Merton by any chance?' Neither recognised the healthy, well filled-out man before their eyes having only known each other as the gaunt, bedraggled, ragged, ill-fed jungle warriors of 1943.

Cozens' intelligence about Japanese numbers in Kanpetlet and Tilin was sent back via the wireless whereas Cozens himself was reliant on runners to Falam. Cozens put him in touch with several Chiefs including the Bumgno Headman, who, despite Cecil's initial suspicions, turned out to be loyal, brave and supportive. A feast was given in their honour and a *mithun* (a cross between a wild bull and a domesticated cow) was slaughtered and served to them. The party was not as enjoyable as the North Chin parties of wild abandon and limitless alcohol. At the South Chin parties the Johnnies were not expected to join in with dancing or singing as they were in the North. So, returning to Shurkhua 'was always like coming home. True it had little more to offer than anywhere else but Van Kio was always so helpful and usually managed to produce some eggs and perhaps a few chickens – stringy little birds.'[6]

Van Kio and all the Chins in the area let Cecil know that they were reluctant to come under Japanese administration as they could see how harsh the Japanese were. However, self-interest and self-preservation came into play to not oppose a Japanese invasion and the reprisals that would follow if they did. They could see that the British forces in the area, the Johnnies and a small force of Levies, were unable to resist an attack and had their valuables hidden in the hills in preparation for flight should the invasion come. Plans were made with Van Kio for a Chin rebellion should the Japanese invade their area. He would move Cecil to a jungle hideout from where he could send intelligence via a trusted Chin liaison officer who would be a relation of Van Kio. When the appointed time came, arms could be dropped by air, to replace the confiscated ancient Chin rifles and rebellion could be fomented.

This plan was vetoed by Delhi and he was ordered to withdraw in this event though he did feel that with the Japanese on the alert for them, hiding was safer than escaping. The spotter planes were very active again and on 29 April it circled very low over Shurkhua for twenty minutes and after that, every morning flying over towards the West or North West.

6 Memoirs/papers of C G Merton IWM/05/11/1.

On 1 May when they were out shooting game for the pot, they saw a small column approaching and were delighted to find that it was his orderly Dum Hpaw Gam with eight porters carrying a supply of rations. He had been forced to abandoned a large amount but had brought all the essentials which included tea, sugar, milk and ghee which gave a lot of pleasure. Not only was Cecil delighted to have all the supplies but also to have a loyal and respected member of the group, as well as a reasonable cook. He also brought spare ammunition and another wireless set, the only thing that Cecil was missing was new footwear as the constant marching was wearing them out. The men were happy to walk barefooted but he never got used to that.

Worried that the regular spotter reconnaissance was a forerunner to invasion, Cecil decided to go down to the plains again and on 6 May, the patrol set off for Migyaung Sakan which was a three-day march away. This time they took a guide from Dunwa village on the instructions of Van Kio and this man was knew his way around the tracks and, most importantly, where to find water. On the march *Havildar* Kya Twa went down with an attack of malaria and was sent back with an escort making the remaining party only four strong. A buffalo had been shot by some Levies, left for a while for fear of alerting the Japanese, then collected and cooked over an open fire. Somewhat putrid and decomposing, they enjoyed the meat feast, nonetheless.

Once on the plains, there was little cover though the trees had sprouted leaves which gave them cover from above. There was no opportunity of hiding or escape from an enemy patrol but on the upside, it also meant there would be no chance of running into a concealed ambush either. Heading east, they set off on a track that Cecil was immediately suspicious about. Every third or fourth tree had a blaze slashed into it, not recent but less than a year old. The Burmese do leave a trail of slashes on the trees but subtly with small slashes well-spaced apart. It was obvious to Cecil that the Japanese had marked this track for some reason, possibly to lead to Trigonometry point 2631 known locally as Kong Tong, a high observation position.

The Johnnies always avoided entering villages but made contact outside the boundaries of the village. Unsure if the villagers were pro-British or pro-Japanese but also very aware of the reprisals that the villagers would suffer if it was known they had assisted the British. It was a no-win situation for the villagers; if they reported a visit, there would be interrogations including slappings, beatings and sometimes executions and if they did not report a visit, the reprisals prompted summary executions. They did, however, enter this village known as Saihaung Taung, having first peered into each house with binoculars. The villagers were most surprised to see them having heard and believed the propaganda that the British had all fled out of India and none were willing to talk to them, or more likely, to be seen talking to them. Money loosened the tongues of two men but the usual drinks were not on offer and they were only able to purchase some eggs. Questioning about the Japanese met a stonewall and it was obvious that these villagers were not to be trusted. After the war Cecil learnt that this village had reported their presence whilst they were still there and a Japanese battalion was sent out immediately to intercept them but it arrived after they had left. On departure, the villagers asked Cecil not to return for fear of reprisals but they did say that they preferred the British who were like 'Mothers and Fathers' to them and they were frightened of the Japanese. They laughed at the idea that the British would re-take Burma from the Japanese.

They returned to Shurkhua on 15 May and two days later Cecil received orders to return to Calcutta having been unable to send messages; one set of batteries would not hold a charge and the other set had been accidently dropped down a hillside, shattering into pieces. After that Cecil had to attach the wireless directly to the charging engine and transmit while the engine was running with great success. However, the charging engine was too heavy to carry on patrols making it unportable. It also had to be carried upright and often the porters forgot this and acid slipped out until the batteries could no longer work properly. On the route home, they came across some disused Japanese camps and picked up old newspapers, maps, cigarette packets and medicine bottles which they sent ahead to IV Corps.

Cecil's *Havildar* had recovered well from his malaria but now Cecil went down with a fever and a poisoned hand. The whole party had swollen faces for about a week as a result of the heat and the bad water they had been drinking from buffalo wallows on the plains. During this week Cecil received information that Parry was ill and would not be returning to the area.

The Chief and his villagers were very sad to say goodbye to the Johnnies and gave them a farewell party and arranged for the storage of as much kit as possible. The Chief promised that in the event of a Japanese invasion, he would hide all the kit in the jungle.

Arriving in Haka on 27 May, Cecil was able to report positively to Turnbull how supportive Chief Van Kio had been to them and that he would like to recommend the Chief for an award in appreciation. A couple more days of marching took him to Falam where he met with Rae before continuing on foot to Trigonometry point 109 at the Indian border near Mualnuan in Manipur State, where he calculated he had marched for 939 miles since leaving Shuganu on 22 February. From here he was able to pick up a Doodlebug (self-propelling train) and then a lorry as far as Imphal where he met up with Parry. Together they proceeded to Calcutta by train and were able to report to Lieutenant Colonel Goring at HQ Eastern Army on 19 June.

Together with his report on the last four and a half months, he made recommendations to set up a guerrilla force in the Chin Hills. His opinion was that the Burmese did not want to be spectators regarding their future and wanted to be a part of the force ejecting the Japanese. Once the Burmese were to see that the British 'meant business, there are a great many who will be anxious to help us eject the Jap.'[7] He also pointed out that there were no large-scale wall maps covering his area at the various headquarters and requested to be posted to an area where he could be of more use.

The arrival of the rains concluded the 'Campaigning Season of 1942-3' where the Johnnies were concerned. Lieutenant General G A P Scoones[8] wrote in a letter dated 10 June 'Now that the monsoon has arrived and the G.S.I.z forward parties, which have been operating in IV Corps, are coming back, I would like at this juncture to express my appreciation of the work which these parties have been doing. I know well enough the hard conditions under which they have been living and operating for weeks on end. I know too the strain that the work imposes on all members of the parties – it has, in fact, been described to my staff by an officer (not a member of one of the forward parties) as similar to hunting a wounded tiger. Despite, however, of the many difficulties with which the parties have had to contend, they have managed to provide a flow of information which has been most valuable to me and had, I think, enabled us to inflict a considerable amount of damage on the Japanese by air action.'[9]

7 Ibid.
8 Lieutenant General Sir Geoffrey Scoones KCB, KBE,DSO,MC (1893-1975), Indian Army, GOC IV Corps, ADC to King George VI, High Commissioner of New Zealand.
9 Lieutenant General Sir Geoffrey Evans, *The Johnnies* (London: Cassell, 1964), p.145.

7

Return to Chin Hills

"If you chose godly honest men to be captains, honest men will follow them."
Oliver Cromwell to Colonel Robert Hammond

During his enforced stay in India, which included a trip to Bombay where Cecil stayed in the Taj Mahal Hotel writing up his report on the previous patrols, Cecil returned to Imphal on 21 August and he was joined there by Parry two days later. They held discussions on when to depart, intending to do so on the 28 August but the road was impassable. They eventually set off on 31 August heading for the Kalemyo Yazagyo area. They passed through Tiddim on 4 September and on to Dimloo, then Dolluang arriving on 13 September. Knowing that the Japanese were occupying the stockades along the Fort White–Kalemyo road, they travelled along jungle tracks through Bhopivum and left a cache of rations in galvanised drums nearby. It was agreed that this would be the rallying point to return to if any members of the patrol were cut off from the others.

On the 20 September they reached a point on the track which gave them an excellent view of Number Two Stockade and with binoculars could watch the Japanese exercising and drilling in their camp. After a ten-mile march down onto the plains, they were fired upon from ahead of them and Cecil and his orderly Dum Hpaw Gam dived behind a bush. Cecil peeked from behind his cover and saw an enemy soldier only twenty yards ahead and had a clear shot until his new Sten gun jammed and he could not remove the cartridge. He whispered to his orderly 'Give me a stick' with which to remove the cartridge. Reloading, the gun jammed a second time but before he could repeat the process, firing came from behind. The Japanese were coming up on their left

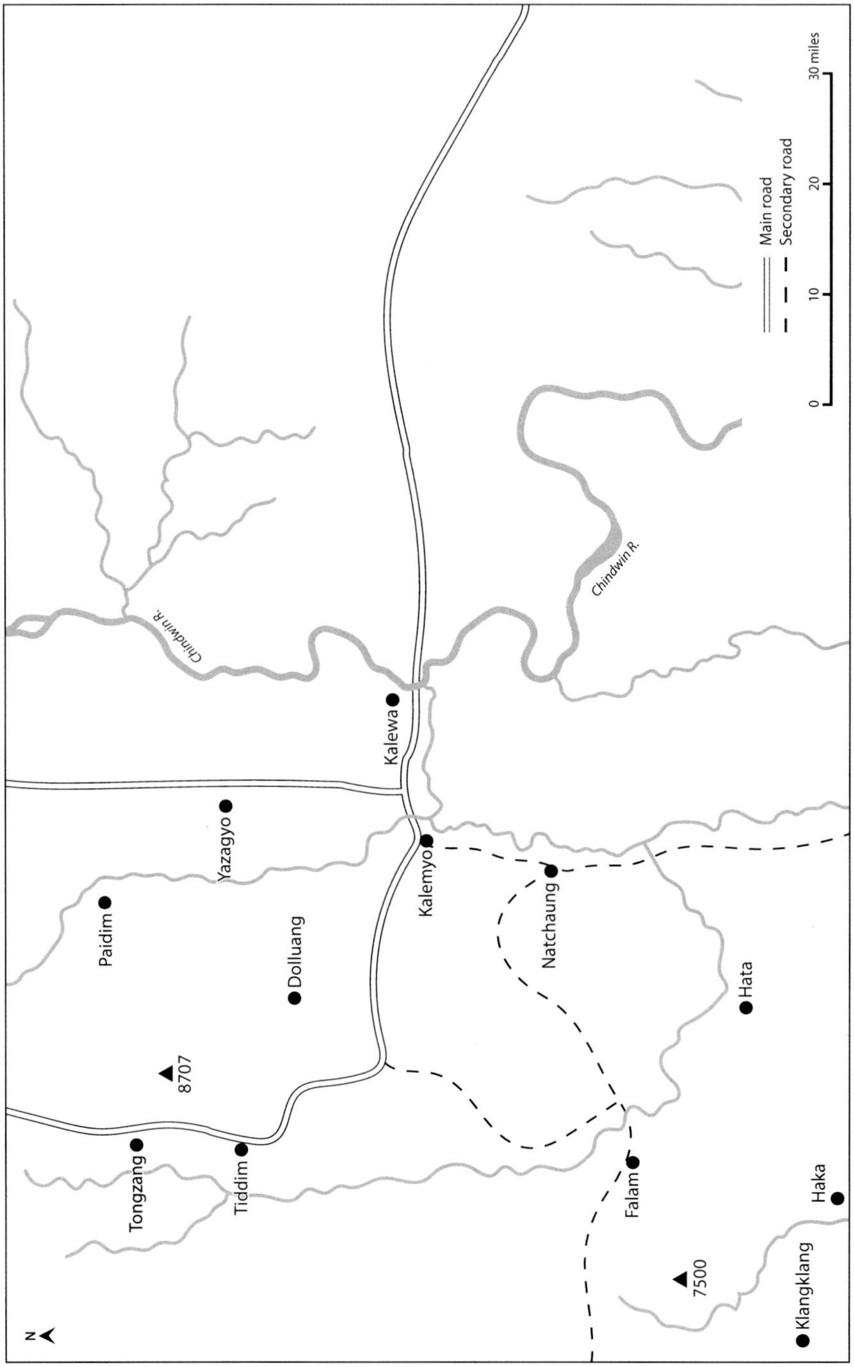

Kalemyo-Dolluang area.

from behind and Parry shouted an order for the patrol to scatter to the right up a steep slope from the track. He made it up the hill without injury and met Parry and they withdrew 100 yards up the track and waited for the rest of the patrol to join them but when they did not appear, they decided to withdraw to the rallying point, meeting some of the men on the way and the rest came in at night fall with the exception of two, Parry's Karen orderly Maung Thein and Cecil's Kachin orderly Dum Hpaw Gam. They waited all the following day for their return and eventually Cecil and a couple of men went back to the site of the fight. They found the remains of a camp with paper wrappings, tins and cigarette packaging from which they estimated meant a force of two or three platoons and their tracks showed they were attempting to encircle the Johnnie's patrol. Footprints headed back along the tracks to Kalemyo and with them went the two orderlies as prisoners. The orderlies persuaded their captors that they were Levies and Dum Hpaw Gam said he was the cook to the Levy officers and was promptly designated cook to the Japanese which meant he received better treatment. He was brought back to the Chin Hills by the Japanese and at one point was close to the cache of rations near Bhopivum and, unobserved, was able to dig up some tobacco for himself.

Returning to their patrol, they set off for the Levy camp outside Suangdaw and camped in the village on the night of 23 September. Three days later Parry left for Tiddim and shortly after, Cecil realised that yet again the wireless was no longer working so he sent a couple of men to catch up with Parry to send it on to Imphal for mending. Soon after Parry had left and the wireless was sent after him, there was heavy firing from the Levy post and Cecil found that they had been attacked by a Japanese force with automatic weapons, whilst the Levies only had one Bren gun, one Tommy gun and the rest of the platoon-strength Levies were armed with vintage rifles. The Chin Levies were most anxious to keep the Japanese from overrunning the village and had moved their families and their belongings into the jungle. The Levies told Cecil that they could not hold off these attacks and must have reinforcements so Cecil borrowed a pony and rode to see the *Subedar* of the Gurkha Commando platoon who were camped nearby. Reluctant to assist as his orders were to hold the junction on the jungle tracks and prevent any enemy advance, he was however from a warring tribe and was 'glad for an excuse to fight'[1] and when

1 Memoirs/papers of C G Merton IWM/05/11/1.

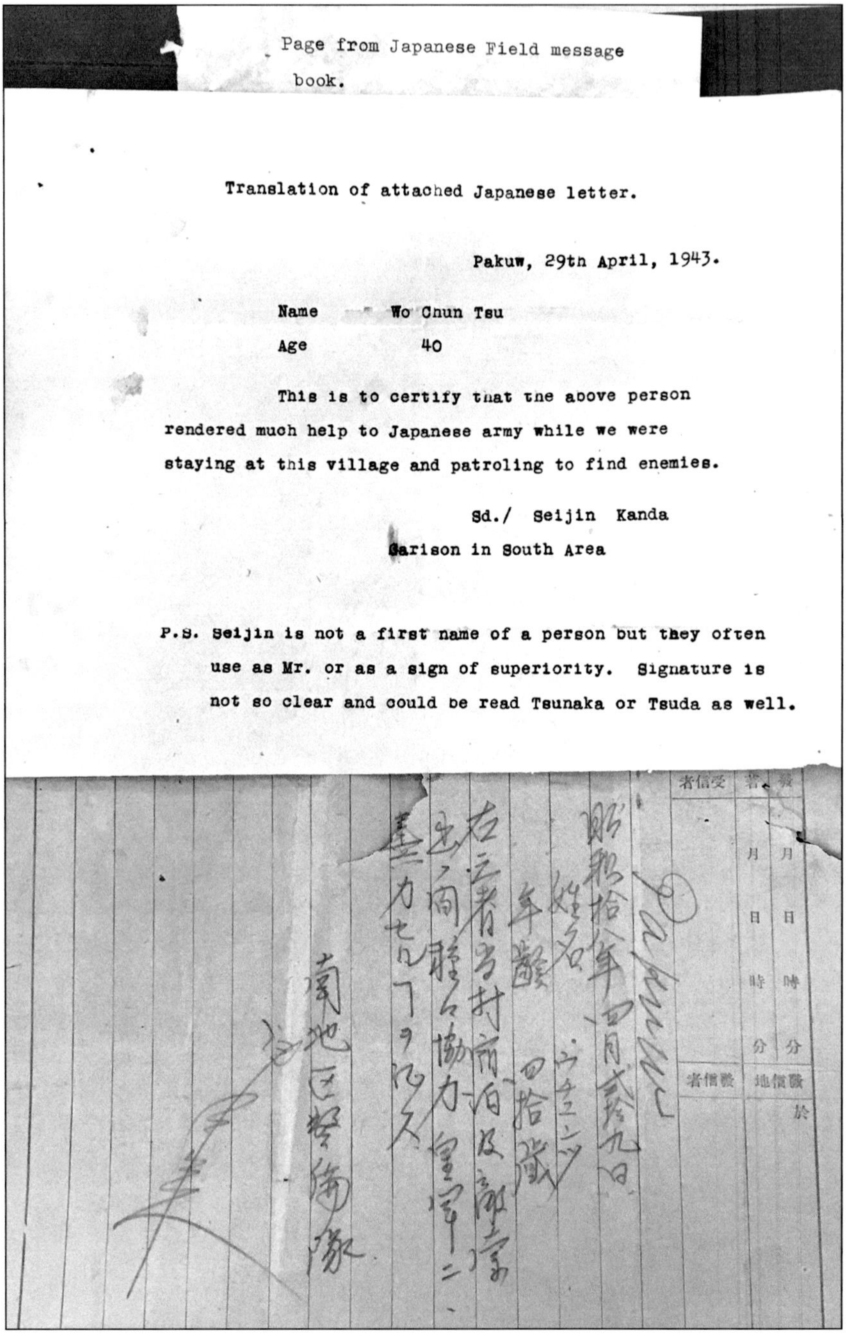

Page from Japanese Field message book.

Translation of attached Japanese letter.

Pakuw, 29th April, 1943.

Name Wo Chun Tsu

Age 40

This is to certify that the above person rendered much help to Japanese army while we were staying at this village and patroling to find enemies.

Sd./ Seijin Kanda

Garison in South Area

P.S. Seijin is not a first name of a person but they often use as Mr. or as a sign of superiority. Signature is not so clear and could be read Tsunaka or Tsuda as well.

Japanese correspondence. (IWM/05/11/1)

Cecil promised to accept responsibility, he agreed to send half his platoon to recapture the Levy post. They had a two-inch mortar gun with them and it was being fired by a gunner standing behind Cecil, whilst he watched the mortar's direction through his binoculars. Only once he had put down the glasses did he realise that the gunner's arm was covered in blood and Cecil's own hat on the floor beside him had a large hole in it. Remarkably no one was severely hurt and the gunner was subsequently awarded the Burma Gallantry Medal. As soon as the enemy firing ceased, they found blood and brains splattered on the trunk of a tree so they knew they had hit at least one casualty. The body had been removed but plenty of Japanese Army biscuits had been scattered around and despite the blood everywhere these were 'quickly devoured on the spot.'[2]

The Gurkhas asked Cecil if he had ever fired a mortar and he was offered a try. The sights were set at an extreme range and he fired a mortar bomb into the distance down the track that the Japanese had disappeared down. The next day a Levy patrol found the body of a dead Japanese, stripped of his uniform by his colleagues and wearing only a pair of underpants. However, a label inside these led to an identification so as Cecil said, 'this small battle gave one important result.'[3]

Parry returned on 2 October and the next day the party moved to near Dolluang. Another Gurkha company position had been established there and when a guide/interpreter was needed for a two-day reconnaissance down to the plains, Cecil volunteered. These Gurkha soldiers were under the impression that Cecil was a GHQ Intelligence Officer recently arrived from Delhi and were not impressed at all with the idea of being guided by a desk-bound GHQ officer. By the end of the two day's reconnaissance, the men asked their own officers if Cecil could be attached to them permanently.

The camp and the village were under continuous attack all through the dry season. The enemy brought up their heavy mortar which was christened 'The Coal Scuttle' … It fired an enormous bomb which came lumbering over but inevitably went clean over our position and landed among the Japs attacking from the other side.'[4]

A shortage of ammunition forced them make the decision to breakout and this was successfully done that evening and they met up with a mule train with

2 Ibid.
3 Ibid.
4 Ibid.

more ammunition and moved on to Tiddim. After a week there Cecil received a message to leave for Imphal but this time he did not have to march out. The improvement in the roads meant he could travel by jeep and did the journey in record time; leaving Tiddim at midday on 19 October and arriving in Imphal at 2300 hours. However, his brand-new Omega self-winding watch could not cope with the shaking on the rough roads and by the time he arrived, the watch had departed this life with a broken spring.

During his meetings in Imphal it was agreed that Cecil and Parry should go north east to the foothills of Yazagyo and the northern end of the Kale Valley and on 22 October, he repeated the journey back to Tiddim before continuing on to between Dollung and Tuisau staying in rather than with the Gurkha camp there. They got to know the 14 Gurkha officers well and enjoyed their time messing with them so it was with great sadness that Cecil later read of the deaths of 12 of them, killed over three days of fighting after the Japanese took Tiddim. 'Every evening with monotonous regularity the Japs would shell our position with one of their guns but it was most ineffective. The gun was perfectly visible near the Dollung school but out of range of any weapons we had there.'[5]

On 15 November they set off with the patrol heading north and after a couple of days marching were able to get transport in jeeps to Tonzang and then onto Khamzang where there was a large Levy post. The Commander, who was an old friend of Cecil, told him that the enemy were occupying the tracks from Sibo and that he could take Levy guides who were local villagers, to show him the tracks and to spot booby traps. There had been some casualties amongst the Levies because of these, but on a positive note, the men had enjoyed feasting on the game which had also set off the traps.

The tracks from Khamzang to Seksih crossed a high-range skirting the Suanglangau Vum (8,000ft) with massive drops to the valley below. The mountaintop was covered in grass, pine trees and rhododendrons with little water. However, when they reached a track junction, they startled a tiger and thinking that he might have had a fresh kill nearby on which they could stock up their meat supply, they investigated where he had appeared from and found a rare drinking hole to fill their bottles from. Pushing onto the otherwise deserted village of Minbil they spotted two men gathering vegetables, who ran

5 Ibid.

off too quickly to be caught but the patrol continued after them and soon came upon an abandoned Levy post. It was obvious that the men had mistaken the Johnnies for the enemy and had alerted their comrades, abandoning what little equipment they had and their evening meal still cooking over the campfire. A free, ready-cooked dinner was much appreciated but realising that the alarm would have been raised, an attack by their own troops was highly possible, they soon left the camp little realising that the Levies had alerted a nearby camp of Commandos from an Indian regiment who came out immediately looking for 'the enemy'. A dangerous week of cat-and-mouse followed and they avoided all tracks apart from the game tracks and cutting cross-country over impossibly high country and valleys. On their arrival in the otherwise deserted village of Sibo, they found a unit of 'B' Levies cooking their evening meal. All the men had put down their weapons to collect wood and water and to light the fire, apart from the Commander who held a Tommy gun. There was excitement on their arrival which Cecil took for pleasure and joined them to eat the cooked venison but after the Levies' departure, patrol members informed him that they had been mistaken for an enemy patrol led by a German officer. A village Headman later told Cecil that he was convinced that the patrol was Japanese and he assumed that they were sent to pretend to be British to test him and see if he would carry out the Japanese orders to report the appearance of any British soldiers. Cecil managed to get him to agree to postpone his report to the Japanese for 48 hours on the condition that Cecil would arrange an airdrop of British leaflets on the village to prove he was who he said he was. This airdrop duly took place.

The tension was still high when they heard people approaching from the West and, worried about trigger-happy soldiers opening fire on them before they could identify themselves there was huge relief to find that it was Parry arriving from Tongzang with the Levy Commander Major Turnbull. He had arrived the 'A' Levy post just after the 'B' Levies had reported the presence of the 'Japanese' in Sibo and a patrol was immediately sent off to investigate. Parry guessed that this 'Japanese advance' was in fact the Johnnies and set off to join them.[6]

6 'A' Levies were ex-Burma Riflemen, trained with British officers. Their role was to fight withdrawing actions with the Japanese, if they advanced, thus gaining time for the regular troops to get into their defensive positions which were difficult to occupy permanently for reasons of supplies mainly water supplies. 'B' Levies were untrained villagers officered

Fearing that their commotion may have alerted the Japanese, they set off on a reconnaissance on 26 November to Paidim in the foothills north west of Yazagyo and observed the enemy going about their business in camp, completely unaware of the Johnnies' presence. With this threat gone for the time being, they returned to Sibo and established an observation post over the Kaba Valley for a week before returning to Tiddim.

Gregory had provided them with a powerful astronomical telescope fitted with a rectifying lens which enabled them to see objects the correct way up at huge distances.

On Christmas Eve they camped in a valley near Mwe Taung which was a high ridge rising 3,000 feet steeply from the Yazagyo Plains. They rarely carried rum but had two bottles and as it was Christmas, they planned to celebrate quietly but there was an outburst of firing nearby. They never discovered the cause of this but assumed that their camp was near a Japanese patrol with a trigger-happy sentry, possibly startled by a wild animal. They hurriedly struck camp and scrambled up the steep hillside in pitch darkness to a spot from where they could defend themselves if attacked. On high alert, no sleep was had that night by anyone and they welcomed Christmas Day from the most spectacular viewpoint over the whole valley. Within a few days an even better observation point was found from where they could watch the Burmese villagers going about their day-to-day life and the arrival of a Japanese foraging party. Through the telescope they could see enemy soldiers strolling down to the river to bathe which proved that the camp could not be far away. The ground between the river and the forested foothills was covered in tall elephant grass making it difficult for them to pinpoint where the camp was but they were soon able to send detailed map references to the RAF. Every evening a map reference was sent of the Japanese bathing spot and where they assumed the camp was located and a flight of Hurricanes flew over bombing and machine-gunning and though the Johnnies could not see the camp, the tell-tale smoke proved that the bombers had hit their target. These continuous, accurate attacks

by their own local leaders, usually junior Headmen. They had limited arms; the leader might have a Tommy gun for prestige purposes and the rest of the men carried their own arms which were mainly muzzle-loading Tawer muskets. The Chin placed high value on arms and the old muskets were spotlessly maintained. The powder was carried in highly decorated horns which were family heirlooms, passed from father to son and impossible to obtain otherwise.

made the Japanese realise they were being watched and soon started sending out patrols. Cecil was just leaving the observation point one evening with two of the men, when shots echoed around the hillside. Impossible to pin-point the source, they quickly hid the telescope and started running towards their hide-out when they spotted two men in the gloom of the evening light. All three made it to their hide-out and a few days later when collecting rice from the village, they heard that a Japanese patrol had surrounded the village as well as surprising some Chin villagers working in a field and had opened fire, capturing three men. The fourth escaped capture as he was collecting water and it was he who told the tale. The Japanese patrol had left the following day taking their prisoners with them.

'After this episode I was very uneasy. I was almost certain that these Chins had a pretty good idea where we were and that the Japanese would not hesitate to use strong measures to force them to tell all they knew. But there was little we could do about it other than to be more vigilant than ever. To this end, I took the precaution to see that throughout the twenty-four hours every man had with him his arms, ammunition and his emergency ration.'[7]

In the whole of the Yazagyo Valley, in their line of vision, there was one solitary tree surrounded by elephant grass and through the telescope Cecil spotted a single sentry concealed within its branches. The following morning a single aircraft made a low pass over the tree strafing its occupant and thirty minutes later twenty or thirty Japanese surrounded the tree and carried away the body. They brought cut boughs from their camp to try and conceal the next sentry but these soon withered away making the next soldier even more visible.

A tiny spring in their hollow allowed them to fill up a four-gallon container overnight and the same by day giving them enough water for cooking and drinking but not washing. However, forty-eight hours of continuous rain allowed them to wash their clothes and bodies for the first time in three weeks. Previously washing was done by leaving a cloth out overnight which was moistened by the dew. None had a change of clothing, apart from their jerseys for the cold, so a chance to wash their clothes with Lifebuoy soap was much appreciated. The bark of the Thayaw creeper also made an excellent shampoo. Only two men at a time were allowed to be naked whilst doing their laundry for fear of an attack, whilst the others manned the perimeter of the camp.

7 Ibid.

One night, Cecil spotted the lights of vehicles moving north. Hard to estimate the numbers from that distance, he fixed the telescope on one point when the lights were visible and keeping it as still as possible was able to count the number of lights on one side of the field of vision. Determining the route of these vehicles was even harder. Looking through the telescope at night showed up the vibrations of the headlights as they bounced along the rough roads but everything else was in total darkness. He tried several different techniques; positioning the telescope on the lights and then looking again in daylight to ascertain the direction or using bamboo sleeves but over a period of two or three days and nights, they were able to establish that the trucks were coming from Kangyi and Kalemyo which would be reached from Pakokku via Pauk and Gangan. He knew this road only too well from 1942 when he had withdrawn along it with 2 Burma Brigade. All of this information was reported back but much later he was to discover that none of it had been believed at the time.

One afternoon the visibility was particularly good and he spotted a light tank crossing a clearing on the far side of the river. Hardly believing his eyes, he spotted one after another despite the fact that tanks had never been seen in the Kabaw Valley before. It dawned on him that he was witnessing the start of an operation of major importance in the valley. He carefully worded his report that night so that there would be no ambiguity and classified it A1 which proved that he had seen it with his own eyes and for which he was in no doubt. Again, he was to discover that Headquarters did not believe his message assuming that he was mistaken. More than a month later when he was in the Tiddim Levy Mess, he was asked if he had 'seen the incredibly funny report on trucks in the Yazagyo Valley – 'Purple trucks with green spots' they had become. Naturally I mentioned that I was the author.'[8]

Cecil hardly left the observation point for days but on 22 January, he received a signal recalling his patrol back to Tiddim at once. He was most reluctant to leave given what was happening in the valley but his orders were to abandon his post immediately, stressing that it was 'most important'. Fearful of being mistaken for the enemy again, he sent off a message giving their route and asking that all units should be notified of their passing by. They left at first light on 24 January, unaware of their narrow escape. Later they discovered

8 Ibid.

that the captured Chins had been forced to give their position away and the camp had been surrounded by 0800 hours on their departure date. As Cecil says 'It was indeed an extremely lucky escape as we would have been caught completely unprepared. Since the alarm I have been more than usually cautious but I was quite certain than we were only in danger of early morning attacks during the full moon and at that time the moon was very low so I reckoned it was impossible for anyone to close in on us during the night.'[9]

On the 25 January on a jungle track, they heard the tramp of boots and dived for cover before realising that it was a British patrol. Fearful of friendly-fire, they let the troops march by, none the wiser of the patrol hidden around them. The message about the Johnnies' movements had been received after this patrol of the West Yorkshires had departed from Salzang.

At Tonzang they met up with Parry who told them the reason for their recall. The army was considering a plan to invade Burma from the West Coast over the Taungou Pass to take place after the rainy season. The invasion was to start in January 1945 but a Z Force patrol would be put in as soon after the rains as possible in December. This patrol would be taken in by submarine to get as close to the coast as possible.

Returning to Tiddim where supplies were stocked up before Parry set out again on patrol, Cecil was staying in one of the messes when he realised that his reports of lorries and tanks were being considered as a figment of his imagination. He held his anger in check.

On 6 February, he returned to Imphal by Jeep and was called into the Intelligence Offices to be cross-examined about the lorries and tank sightings. He said that 'the tanks were not referred to; no doubt being regarded as the product of an over stimulated imagination or I had only chanced one very brief view of them but the lorries I had reported nightly for more than two weeks. I was asked if I was sure I wasn't mistaken – no doubt I had seen lights but couldn't it have been villagers with electric torches. I pointed out that it was impossible for so many people to have the batteries by this time and in any case were in pairs and vibrating violently like the lights of a lorry jerking over a rough road.'[10]

9 Ibid.
10 Ibid.

It was suggested that they were bullock carts with petrol lamps. He offered to take a staff officer back to the observation post but this offer was not accepted. After three days he was beginning to doubt his own eyes and memory but on the fourth summons there were apologies all round as his story had been corroborated by a Burmese prisoner of the Burma National Army (BMA) who under interrogation, stated he had seen many loaded lorries pass through Yazagyo every night heading for a position a mile north-west of the village. At last his story was believed and was considered, finally, a most valuable piece of intelligence.

On 13 February Cecil flew to Comilla and was interviewed by Army Headquarters about his opinions of a potential Japanese attack. He told them that he expected the Japanese occupying 'Fort White would punch straight into Tiddim through Kennedy Peak and would use a pincer movement against Tonzang from Yazagyo and mile 109 from Fort White by way of Mualbem track from Fort White crossing by Kapitec and Mualnuam to attack Tonzang on MS 109 from the South West.'[11]

He felt that no one was very interested at the time but was told later by Toby Shuttleworth that one of the officers present had told him that a visiting Intelligence Officer had 'foretold almost exactly the movements of the Japs were actually to make when they launched their Imphal offensive.'[12]

On 14 February Cecil flew to Calcutta and then by train to Delhi where he discussed plans for his next patrol. He met several of Mountbatten's staff and the plans for the submarine were discussed at length. The Burmese Government was in Simla so on 28 February Cecil went there to arrange a 'passport' or 'letter of introduction' as well as meetings in Signals Headquarters regarding a special wireless which used transistors rather than valves and fitted into an aluminium box. He presented his credentials to the Burmese Government Intelligence Bureau.

Flying back to Delhi on 5 March, armed with his letter of introduction, he was pleased with how all the preparations had gone and soon a communication arrived from the Navy giving him three weeks to get ready as after that the weather conditions would be unsafe. Colonel Shelley exploded with anger, the only time Cecil ever saw him do so, concerned with getting the

11 Ibid.
12 Ibid.

patrol back onto the submarine if there was only such a short weather window. He immediately cancelled the patrol and Cecil realised what a difficult assignment it would have been. 'Since fate had called it off, I felt it would probably have had fateful results for us if we had gone.'[13]

With this plan scrapped, Cecil flew to Calcutta on 16 March to discuss the alternatives for the next patrol. It was to go into Indaw Nabh/Katha area in April and the thought of this pleased Cecil hugely as it might mean news of Minny and the children. The plan was to use one of Wingate's bases as a Headquarters and to operate from there. Cecil immediately volunteered.

Preparations for his patrol involved a couple of trips to Comilla and Sylhet and while he was preparing, the news came through of the air crash that had killed Wingate. 'Wingate was dead. His aircraft had flown into the side of a mountain near Bishenpur, and he had been killed instantly. It said only that he had been

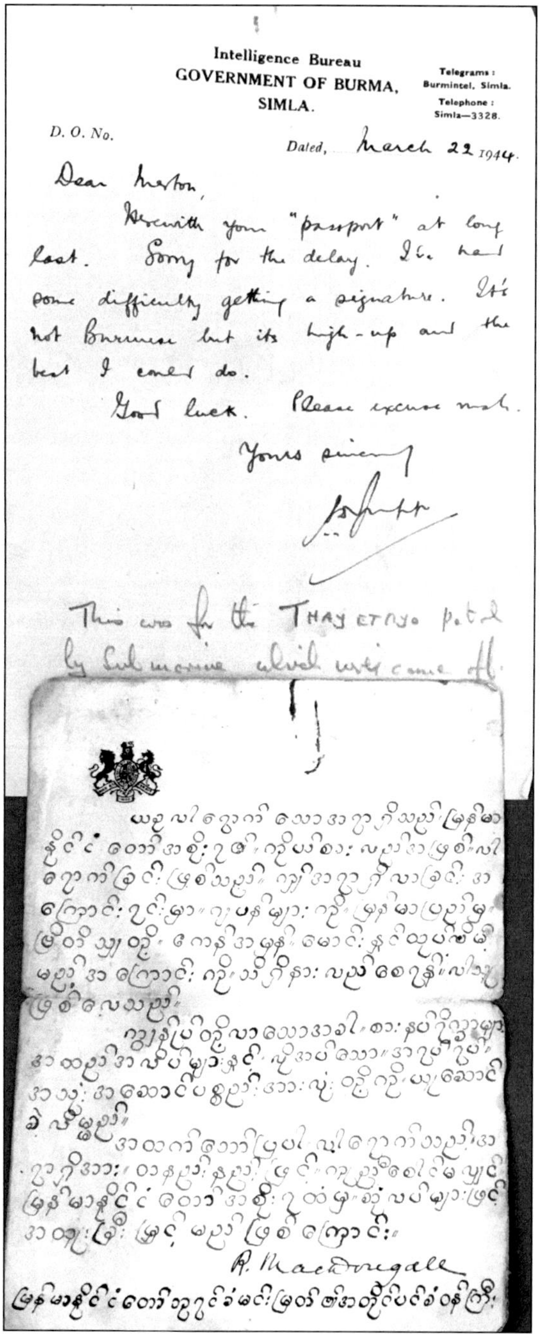
Intelligence Bureau
GOVERNMENT OF BURMA,
SIMLA.

Telegrams: Burmintel, Simla.
Telephone: Simla—3328.

D. O. No.

Dated, March 22 1944.

Dear Merton,

Herewith your "passport" at long last. Sorry for the delay. I've had some difficulty getting a signature. It's not Burmese but it's high-up and the best I could do.

Good luck. Please excuse rush.

Yours sincerely

This was for the THAYETMYO patrol by submarine which was came off.

R. MacDougall

Passport. (IWM/05/11/1)

13 Ibid.

missing for five days and was believed killed and that Joe Lentaigne would take over command of the Force when he could be flown out from his own Brigade.'[14] It was General Joe Lentaigne that Cecil lunched with when he went to Sylhet to discuss future patrols.

As Yamauchi's Fifteenth Army commenced its advance north to the Manipur border and Sato's 31st Division headed for Nagaland, Parry and his men silently slipped across the border into the Lushai Hills and to safety. The battles ahead in Kohima, Imphal and Admin Box were to be the turning points of the war in Burma.

'I did hear a story afterwards which I should like to think was true but I will never know. It is said that Mountbatten questioned Slim on the wisdom of leaving his Eastern flank unprotected and suggested that he should deploy a division in the Shan Hills for this purpose. Slim is supposed to have replied that his flank was quite secure as it was being watched by a Z patrol. If this story is true then we had good reason to feel that we were doing something useful – ten men replacing a division. Actually, I don't suppose there was any truth in the story but anyhow this new role was good for our morale which was getting a little low'[15] Cecil observed after his return from this patrol.

14 Fergusson, Brigadier Bernard, *The Wild Green Earth* (London: Collins, 1946), p.117.
15 Ibid.

8

Aberdeen

> "The war in Burma was a soldier's war."
>
> Field Marshal Viscount Slim

Cecil spent several weeks in preparation, expecting to return to the Chin Hills but the Japanese attacks on Tiddim caused their patrol to be put on hold. He had meetings with Lieutenant Colonel Edwards at Intelligence Headquarters in Comilla and after a considerable delay waiting for some of the patrol to return with Parry and re-equip them, they were able to start out on 23 April heading for 3rd Indian Division Headquarters in Sylhet. They finally arrived at Aberdeen, near Indaw on 25 April. This was the 'Stronghold' of Brigadier Bernard Fergusson,[1] Brigade Commander of Column 5 of Wingate's Chindits, however, it was decided to move into Haunghmi Village rather than the camp itself as being in an inhabited village gave them more contact with the locals. Before they left Aberdeen, the staff there, impressed with what the Johnnies were doing, gave them the freedom of their stores to take whatever they wanted. They were offered de-brayed mules but decided to only take two shotguns and some cartridges with which to shoot game for the pot.

Cecil's first job was to visit Lieutenant Colonel Upjohn, the Fort's commanding officer, with his proposals. Upjohn was fairly unenthusiastic about the patrol's chances of survival as well as gaining useful intelligence with the impending withdrawal of the strongholds. Cecil knew nothing about the withdrawals and that completely upset his plans to hide up for the monsoon.

1 Brigadier B E Fergusson, DSO, KT, GCMG, OBE (1911-80), Black Watch, ADC Wavell 1936-39, GSO Middle East, JPS Delhi 1942, 77 Indian Brigade, Governor-General of New Zealand 1962-67.

It would be impossible to hide up on the plains without a secure base where men could recuperate from the illnesses that abounded there. As his intention was to obtain intelligence from the Irrawaddy Valley, he decided to change his plans for the south and to go north-east into the hills to hide up. The villagers there were friendly, the area reasonably healthy and close to the railway which ran north-south and with contact on the Mansi Plain. Colonel Upjohn thoroughly approved of this plan. Captain Smythies,[2] Civil Affairs officer with 16 Brigade, heard of his plan and asked to remain with the Johnnies when his Column returned to India. Cecil dispatched the following message:

> *27.4.44*
> *'My present position is at Aberdeen (.) Owing friends immediate movements now impossible operate South (.) Must have good base for monsoon where can rest if ill (.) Local comd considers it now impos operate South (.) Propose make base in Kachin area map ref SG 76 (.) Healthy hills (.) All villagers speak Burmese and have Kachins in party (.) They very friendly and have helped our troops in the past when in difficulty (.) They have contact with railway villagers affording very good opportunity for getting valuable long term intelligence from South (.) Excellent cover for entry to area given by friends whom can accompany and then leave them on arrival in desired area (.) Jap would not know we have remained (.) Access to area easy now but would be impos later from India (.) CAS Officer Captain Smythies who knows area and had contacts wishes join me (.) Arrange immediately temporary release at his request (.)'*[3]

Cecil noted that he took steps to hide the Johnnies' identity and never disclosed that they had a wireless, always going to the Fort to send messages and letting himself be known by a false name amongst the villagers.

The Shan Burmans of Haunghmi and the surrounding villages were very friendly, bringing the chickens and playing games with the men of the patrol but all were cautious of speaking their minds. They said that they knew who was pro-British and who was Pro-Japanese but declined to name names fearing reprisals.

2 Captain Bertram Evelyn Smythies (1912-99), read Botany and Forestry at Balliol, Burma Forest Service, Commissioned 1943, Major 1946, Mentioned in Dispatches for 'gallant and distinguished services in Burma'. Ornithologist. Author *The Bird Book of Burma.*

3 Memoirs/papers of C G Merton IWM/05/11/1.

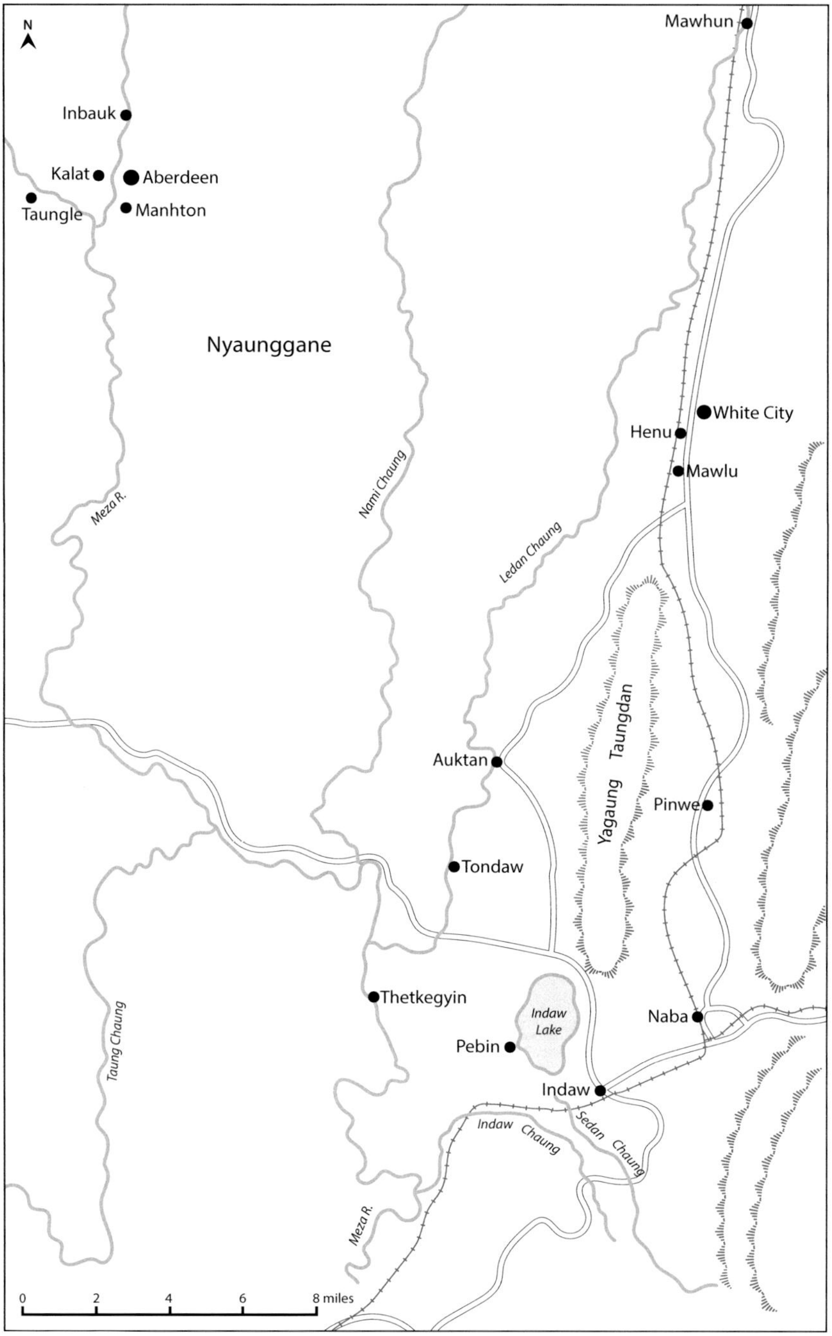

Aberdeen-Indaw area.

A small party of sick and wounded Chindits with an Army Chaplain passed through on their way to their flights out of Aberdeen. One of the soldiers had died and the Padre, who did not speak any Burmese languages, asked Cecil to arrange the funeral. The Padre watched as the men piled thorns on top of the shallow grave and asked why this was done. Cecil explained that it was to keep the spirits in, 'and the dogs out' thought the Padre.[4]

After receiving every possible assistance from Colonel Upjohn, the Johnnies left Aberdeen on the evening of 29 April and proceeded up the Meza River spending the night in Budaung village before marching up river to Pakaw where they spent the night in the Headman's spare hut. The following morning Major Webster of Z Force passed through the village with his patrol. He thought the idea of Cecil's hiding up was a very good one and would provide valuable intelligence but feared the army would not endorse it. For the next few days Cecil and Smythies reconnoitred the area working out where to leave food dumps and were pleased to find a suitable hide-out well situated off the beaten track. It was on a hillock, well drained, sunny and well-concealed as secrecy was the order of the day. He did not want any villagers knowing where he was nor having porters deliver stores to the camp. He recruited unmarried, reliable men from the two villages and they alone would know the camp's whereabouts. These men would live in the camp only visiting their villages once a week to collect intelligence.

Cecil considered that he would be able to obtain very valuable intelligence if his patrol was to remain behind during the rains but on 6 May when out with his patrol, he received an executive signal from Comilla which read: *'Army order you withdraw back to India immediately with help of Number 3 who will render any assistance to whole party (.) If now detached contact column proceeding north as per last message.'*[5]

Distributing the supplies that they would be unable to carry amongst the villagers, the patrol set off on 8 May for Haungpa but not before asking the Headman of each village to continue providing intelligence in their absence, and to pass it to the nearest Station Master.

Cecil was very aware of possible Japanese reprisals towards the Kachin villagers. The enemy knew that one hundred rifles had been distributed amongst

4 Ibid.
5 Ibid.

Pro-British villagers and had written a letter demanding that these rifles were to be handed in or the population would be exterminated. Penned by a Kachin, the letter expressed amazement that the Kachins were Pro-British as this was a war of East v. West and called upon the Kachins to join the Brotherhood of the East, uniting to drive out the British and Americans. 'Asia for the Asians'.

On their way through the small village of Hpagla, they were asked for medical assistance for the Headman. His painful back made walking difficult and was passing blood in his stools. This was the result of a severe beating by the Japanese because of the presence of two Karen riflemen left behind from Wingate's first expedition in 1943. The two riflemen escaped but the Headman and his brother were beaten with a heavy stick. The brother who was suffering from malaria at the time, died from his injuries leaving a widow and four young children. Cecil recommended this family for a pension as well as a reward to the Headman to encourage further assistance of stragglers from the 1944 Chindit expedition.

A villager from Ngagyan village told Cecil that he had been badly beaten for owning a rifle and accused of owning a service revolver too. He was knocked unconscious and taken to Mornyin Jail where he was given no food or water for five days.

On 14 May the patrol arrived in Nansang after a tiring march in intense heat through 'the worst leech country I have ever seen.'[6] Cecil had been suffering from a fever since 11 May and at times on the march they had at least 20 leeches attached to them at a time. Every time they crossed the river, they would stop and remove the leeches but after walking a hundred yards or so, they would have to stop and remove another twenty leeches. The loss of blood and the attacks of malaria meant that all the men were struggling and Cecil was worrying about being able to sleep at night with the leeches. He had not heard at the time but several of the stragglers from Wingate's first Chindit expedition had gone to sleep and not woken up having been drained of blood by leeches.

There was an American camp here, an outpost of their 101 Organisation (OSS Detachment)[7] and they were very welcoming to the Johnnies. A message was sent to Colonel Cochrane's Air Commandos in Taro requesting planes to

6 Ibid.
7 Office of Strategic Services – initially 21 members activated in April 1942 led by Major Carl Eifler (1906-2002) known as 'The deadliest Colonel'.

fly them out but Taro were unable to help but some light planes bringing in Kachin reinforcements agreed to fly some of the sicker, weaker members of the party. Ahead of them was a seven-day march at the beginning of the monsoon, no villages to stay in and many of the men suffering from malaria. Not looking forward to this final march, 'It really looked as though we were at last going to be faced with the problem of deciding whether to risk the whole patrol in trying to extricate any member who went sick on the way or to abandon him to die or, even more difficult, to carry out a mercy execution.'[8] Cecil was hugely relieved when the pilots of the light aircraft insisted on coming back to fly the remainder out, on their own initiative. Flown into Taro, they were greeted with full-blown American hospitality; a bottle of whiskey, American cigarettes, a complete change of uniform and outstanding non-ration meals to build up their strength over the next five days of recuperation. There was a jolly Warrant Officer called Pop Warfield from Texas, who said he was a cousin of Wallis Warfield Simpson, whose speciality was Barbequed Suckling Pig and this was laid on in their honour.

So, the pre-Monsoon 1944 patrol came to a premature end and the Johnnies did not have to sit out the rains in their concealed camp in 3rd Irrawaddy Division Box area. The group of three Karens, one Burma Gurkha, two Kachins, two Chins, one Burman, Cecil and Smythies were planning to sit it out until August but if they had to withdraw before that they would have been replaced by a 'Sittaing Johnnie', a forest officer from the Katha area that Cecil does not name but thinks highly of.

8 Ibid.

9

Chindwin Patrol

> "Go, tell the Spartans, thou who passest by, that here obedient to their laws – we lie."
>
> Simonides of Ceos, Cenotaph of Thermopylae

After attending a conference in Simla where the clandestine patrols were reorganised, Cecil returned to Calcutta as Quartermaster in charge of the massive quantities of stores, as well as sourcing and arranging padding to surround a new ration pack. During this time a signal came through requesting two patrols to complete a reconnaissance of the Chaungzauk area, east of the Chindwin reporting on Japanese troop movements from Schwebo. It was not known if they were in full retreat after their defeat at Imphal or whether they were 'reinforcing for a new offensive when the open season commenced in November.'[1]

Various methods were discussed. General Scoones suggested a fighting patrol of African troops carrying folding boats that would escort them across the river and then return with the boats leaving the Japanese none the wiser but finally it was agreed that they would fly in by glider and dismantle them on landing so as not to be spotted by enemy air reconnaissance.

On 24 September Wood and Cecil travelled by air to Imphal and arrangements were made with IV Corps Headquarters for three planes and three gliders which duly arrived, whilst Cecil was trying to map out suitable landing sites for the gliders 'but those were few and far between in this jungle country.'[2] There was a glider for each patrol and one in reserve and the pilots would

1 Memoirs/papers of C G Merton IWM/05/11/1.
2 Ibid.

have to join the patrol once landed. They had had no briefing on the nature of their mission and Cecil was amazed when they turned up in normal uniforms, wearing shoes with no concept of the weeks ahead, 'foot-slogging with a heavy pack.'[3]

A secret meeting took place at Tully Hall airstrip and a pilot called Buchanan was singled out as the most suitable of the pilots, he was the most enthusiastic about joining the team and the patrol needed a 2 IC. Buchanan was kitted out with rubber boots and jungle kit whilst preparations were made and reconnaissance flights were undertaken in Mosquitoes, to find a suitable landing site for the gliders but both Wood and Cecil found that the planes flew too fast for them to see properly. Dress rehearsals were undertaken to practise remote releases to ascertain the weight of the loaded glider as well as night-time take-offs. Eventually, the plans for gliders were abandoned in favour of trucks.

Meanwhile, in the Chin Hill, Newland and Rae who were two miles south of Haka, heard a rumour of a Japanese advance on 8 October. Levies in Hata, North-East of Haka, were attacked. Falam was evacuated at the beginning of November and Haka occupied on 12 November. The Japanese occupiers burned, thieved and raped through every town and village.

The ground around the Rest House was littered with the skeletons of refugees from 1942 and the more recent corpses of Japanese soldiers. It is thought that that is where Wood caught his nearly fatal attack of Scrub Typhus which abruptly ended his patrol of Kabaw Valley and put him in hospital in Imphal for weeks.

Memories of the Retreat in 1942 were strong as Cecil and his patrol marched along the road towards Tamu, remembering how 2 Burma Rifles formed the rear guard as they approached the Lochchoo River crossing. This time they were in trucks which each got bogged in mud in turn and the first twenty miles to Pyenbum Salom took an entire day. Each truck had a winch which allowed them to extract themselves with slow but comparative ease. The trucks were left behind at Pyenbum Salom and they set off on foot for Sittaung and, borrowing boats from the villagers, crossed the Chindwin to Mogaung. They were to spend four days in that village recruiting guides, porters and sending out parties to bury the Japanese corpses that lay everywhere.

3 Ibid.

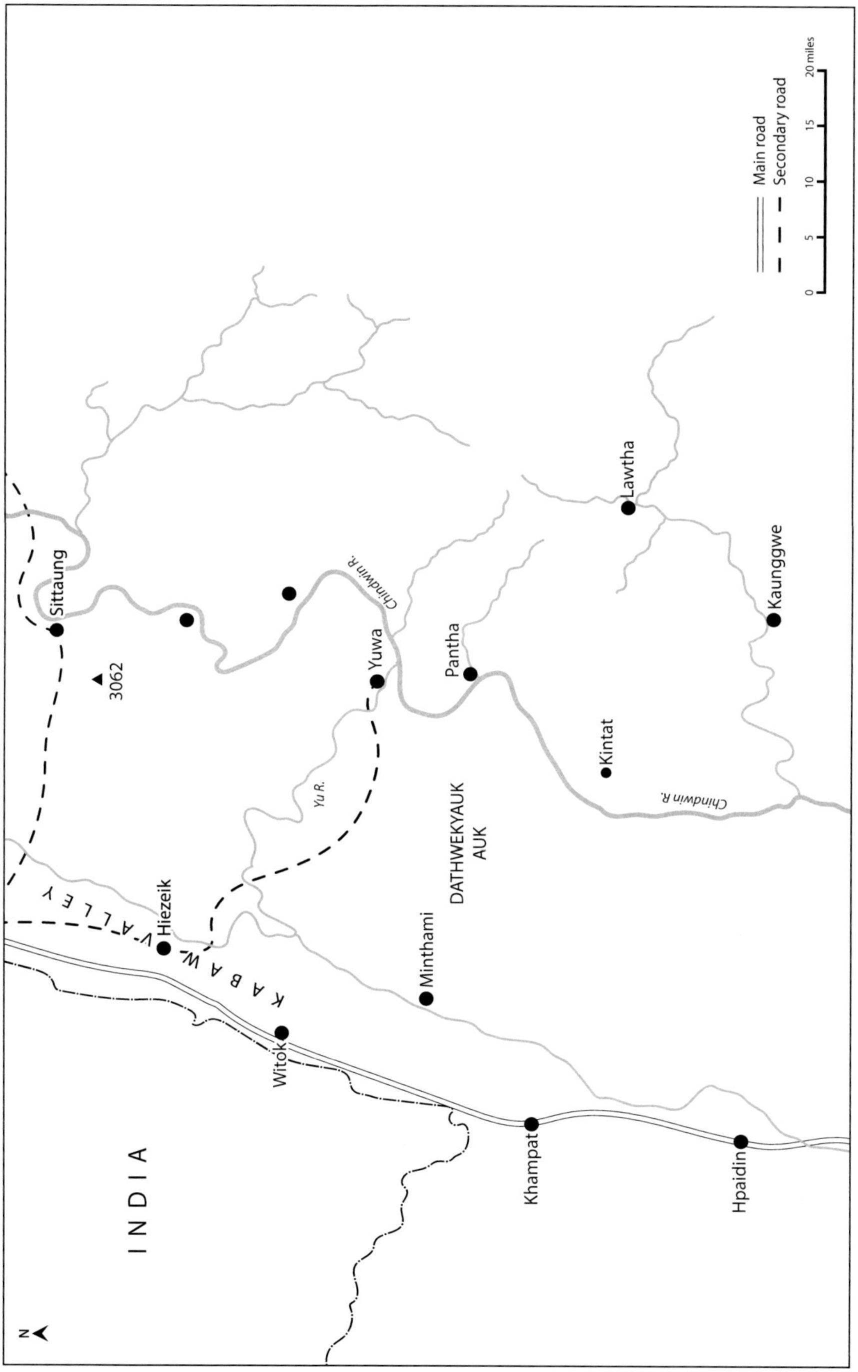

Chindwin-Lawtha area.

A Dakota drop of rice, salt and clothing was made before they set off on 15 October, heading south avoiding the established tracks so as to not bump into Japanese patrols from Pale and Naubon. However, not using tracks was very slow work and eventually they put caution aside and continued on the existing tracks.

A party of villagers confirmed that there were 1500 Japanese in Pahe which was four miles to the east. Asked how they knew this, the party replied that they were returning from delivering vegetables to the Japanese camp. The patrol was to receive an airdrop of rations which Cecil describes as 'luxury'. One parachute load was caught high up in a tree and Tai Cawn climbed up to retrieve the cannister but was unable to get the yellow and blue canopy down from the highest branches so the tell-tale evidence was left hanging.

To avoid interception, the patrol walked barefoot, as none of the villagers had rubber boots or shoes, following the *chaung* bed, clambering exhaustingly over large log piles left on the banks by the Bombay Burma Trading Company.

The rains were still pouring down but they had new jungle hammocks which kept them cosy, though there were nights when, wary of Japanese patrols hearing the zip fasteners, they were unable to use them properly and spent nights thoroughly wet through.

Despite Cecil's years in the country, he was amazed to find how different this landscape was. 'Had been in the Chin Hills before – but this was really Burma.'[4]

The area to the south of Lawtha was very dry with badly eroded low hills. The country was intersected with countless *chaungs* and gullies with deep beds and vertical banks making crossings impossible in places. Few landmarks made it hard to determine one's location for airdrops.

Cecil decided that he needed a local guide from the village of Lawtha. Approaching the village, they hid up until evening when a pair of villagers walked by and giving them a couple of gold coins, promised them more if the village Headman would come and talk to them. One of the men was silent, the other very verbose, offering accommodation in the village. Declining this, the patrol moved further back along the track to a point where they could see an approaching enemy force if needed. The following day, the same silent man appeared, much agitated and nervous and told them that the talkative man was

4 Ibid.

the Pro-Japanese Headman of the village and he had reported their presence to the platoon of Japanese in their village who had sent to Indaw for reinforcements who would be searching for them at present. The quiet man said he had waited all day for an opportunity to slip out without being noticed, to warn the patrol of this danger. Thanking the man, they hastily retreated to put several miles between themselves and the village and did not camp until well after dark. This meant that they were unsure of their position the following morning when they set off again at dawn. Boot prints in a *chaung* bed showed that a Japanese patrol were out looking for them, so they pushed on south to the village of Sabet to the east of Indaw where they were to receive another supply drop. There was open space for the drop so they lit their fire by the shallow river to alert the planes who released four parachutes and their cannisters. The area was at the furthest range of the 'Hurry'[5] bombers, taking off from Imphal and refuelling at Palell.

A member of the patrol had a close escape entering the village of Sabet where he had a contact. Cecil noticed that he was using a piece of parachute cord as a belt and removed it, checking thoroughly through his bags and removing more parachute silk kept as a trophy. On entering the village, the two patrol members encountered a Japanese patrol who seized them, accused them of being agents for the British and searched them thoroughly, but found nothing to arouse their suspicions and the tale of visiting a village friend was corroborated. They were released after being told to look out for the Johnnies' tracks and being promised a reward for information leading to their capture. They returned to the patrol the following evening with an extra couple of men, to the huge relief of the Johnnies. The men with them were traders whose legitimate business allowed them to travel far afield and one had just returned from Schwebo and was able to give Cecil quite a lot of useful information. They immediately offered to act as agents, but not as guides and confirmed that the established tracks were too dangerous to travel on and that the rest of the country was almost impossible to traverse.

Cecil then went down with a bad fever and knew that he had to rest up for a while, fully aware that their safety depended on keeping moving. They never knew if the agents they recruited were also working for the enemy and at any moment could bring a Japanese patrol into their camp. 'It is when we

5 Hawker Hurricane bombers.

stay in camp that we are most vulnerable. Life was too stressful for all of us and we were too small a party to be able to afford sentries except under exceptional circumstances.'[6] Knowing that 'trampled grass and undergrowth in the jungle and footprints in the sand were our give away',[7] they spent the next five hours splashing up the stream until they found a small tributary which allowed them to scramble up the rocks to a ridge where they could rest up until Cecil's malarial fever passed. Their tracks had 'disappeared' miles back so there was nothing to guide any pursuing patrols to their current hide out and they waited in their hammocks until darkness when they could cook their food. 'One can hide the flames of a camp fire but not the smoke.'[8] Dosed on malarial drugs and aspirin; Cecil remained there for the next three days. On the fourth day, he felt better and with rations running low, he signalled for an airdrop in a suitable spot. Once rations were replenished, they continued their visits to villages to recruit agents with some considerable successes. At one village, the Headman came out accompanied by another man who immediately fell to his knees, touched his head on the ground and said that Cecil could kill him then and there. He stammered in a desperate manner, tongue-tied and terrified but gradually his story was told. He had previously been a political *pongyi* (priest) but had discarded his robes and thrown in his lot with the Japanese and until two weeks previously had been in charge of a convoy of elephants delivering food and cash to Japanese camps in the neighbourhood. After the Japanese defeat at Imphal, he had run away, been recaptured and managed to run away again. He knew he would be executed by the Japanese if captured again and fully expected the same fate from the British so did not know which way to turn but threw himself on Cecil's mercy. Despite suspicions, Cecil decided to trust him, 'we had nothing to lose if we took him in and perhaps a lot to gain'[9] and they pored over maps with him pointing out the positions of Japanese camps; numbers of troops in each and where all the hidden ammunitions and arms were. This was all passed on to Imphal and the RAF who were able to bomb and strafe these camps. Intelligent and articulate (when not under stress), he could read a map and had an excellent memory for the position of all the Japanese camps

6 Ibid.
7 Ibid.
8 Ibid.
9 Ibid.

allowing Cecil to pin-point six of them, containing between 500 and 1500 Japanese, with a six-figure map reference. One target that he gave Cecil was some Japanese artillery that the enemy had brought back across the Chindwin from the defeat of Imphal. They were concealed from ariel bombing being hidden in a hole dug into the side of a hill across the river, but not for long thanks to a commando raid. XXXIII Corps Headquarters became very interested in him and Cecil received a signal asking him to bring the man in and hand him over to the Field Security Officer being sent out for his interrogation. Army Headquarters took exception to this interference and Cecil received a signal addressed to XXXIII Corps stating that it was 'entirely at Major Merton's discretion whether he handed him over or not'. 'Actually, we all became so fond of him, he was always so willing to do any odd job that I eventually availed myself of this authority and declined to hand him over to Corps where he might have come in for less sympathetic treatment than we felt he deserved, especially as, when nervous he used to stutter so much that he became tongue tied so I took him back to Imphal with me when I went and let Intelligence there interrogate him to their heart's content, myself acting as interpreter.'[10]

Eventually Cecil took him to a Burma Refugee Camp where he knew he would be well treated and arranged for him to be the recipient of a small Z Force pension as 'he had served us excellently and I am sure he had committed no real crime. True he had been a collaborator but that was due only to misdirection.'[11]

Another member of the patrol was a baby monkey that had been caught by one of the men. Cecil felt that it was harmless enough to allow Kya Twe to keep it. One day as they were walking down a wide sandy river with very little water in it, staying in the water to avoid leaving footprints, they rounded a corner straight into a column of men. The patrol dived into the elephant grass convinced that they had been seen by a Japanese patrol but turned out to be Burmese villagers taking their goods to market in Wuntho by rail. The poor monkey had been thrown off the shoulders of Kya Twe and began to screech hysterically and so had to be released into the wild to silence him and he ran away howling. The two hundred villagers were talking so much that they had

10 Ibid.
11 Ibid.

not even noticed the commotion. Their village was several days walk away and they had no useful intelligence to impart but the leader of the party volunteered to collect information on troop movements in their area.

After ordering another airdrop by the river, the patrol met some villagers cutting bamboo and one of them was the Headman of Tunnein Village who was most cooperative and friendly. He informed Cecil that the British had crossed the Chindwin and there were troops 20 miles away in Nyaunglintha and that Japanese activity had greatly increased recently. A patrol had visited his village and another would be visiting that day. He said that the Japanese had made some sort of stronghold and that his village had been forced to help which allowed him to give Cecil very detailed descriptions of the fortifications as well as the exact location. The very location was exactly where the patrol's airdrop was due and Cecil hastily cancelled the supply drop and ordered a bombing raid instead.

Hearing that their own troops were advancing was a huge morale boost for the 'jubilant' patrol but the close proximity of enemy patrols meant no local camp that night and they marched well past darkness and wearily pitched their camp close to the track and started cooking their evening meal when they heard the approaching footsteps of a man and two women. Suspicions were aroused by their shifty demeanour. A search of the man's bag produced a notebook with a list of names headed by that of a well-known *pongyi* called U Konthia that Z Force officer Willy Goldberg had been trying to capture since 1942. The man tried to pass off the list as people who owed him money but *pongyis* do not handle money, so this made Cecil more suspicious still. Although prisoners were a real hinderance, they took these three with them, tied together with parachute cord and each man took turns to do sentry duty. They took the prisoners to Nyaunglintha but not before they narrowly missed bumping into a Japanese patrol. 'If we had been able to find a suitable place to lunch as we had intended, we must surely have bumped into them. One more instance of the divine providence which seemed to be protecting us.'[12]

They had planned to reach the British lines by night-time but did not manage to do so, so camped in a circle with the prisoners in the centre with a sentry on guard. This time it was not the enemy but a leopard who circled their camp all

12 Ibid.

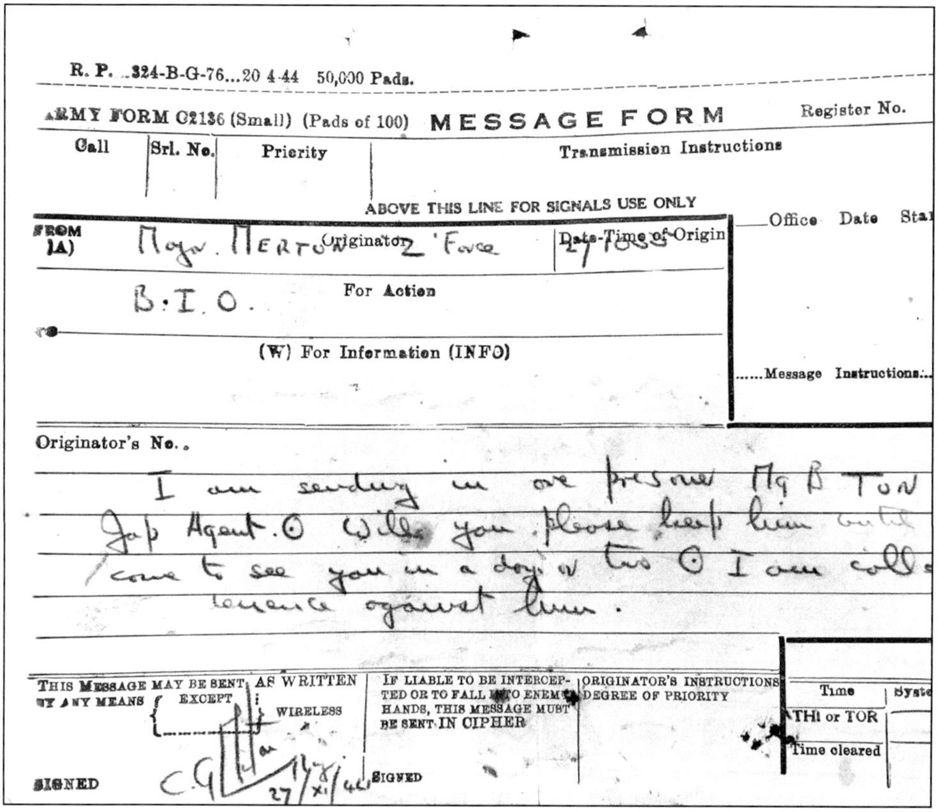

R. P. ..324-B-G-76...20 4-44 50,000 Pads.

ARMY FORM C2136 (Small) (Pads of 100) MESSAGE FORM Register No.

Call | Srl. No. | Priority | Transmission Instructions

ABOVE THIS LINE FOR SIGNALS USE ONLY

FROM (A) Originator Maj. Merton's Force Date-Time of Origin 27 1800 | Office Date Sta

TO B.I.O. For Action

(W) For Information (INFO) | ......Message Instructions...

Originator's No.

I am sending in one prisoner Mg B Ton
Jap Agent. Will you please keep him until
come to see you in a day or two. I am coll-
-ence against him.

THIS MESSAGE MAY BE SENT AS WRITTEN BY ANY MEANS EXCEPT WIRELESS | IF LIABLE TO BE INTERCEPTED OR TO FALL INTO ENEMY HANDS, THIS MESSAGE MUST BE SENT IN CIPHER | ORIGINATOR'S INSTRUCTIONS DEGREE OF PRIORITY | Time | Syste THI or TOR | Time cleared

SIGNED C.G. ... 27/xi/44 | SIGNED

Telegram. (IWM/05/11/1)

night, they heard his 'cough' from first one direction and then the next, and so none of the patrol or their prisoners had a moment of sleep that night. Despite the lack of sleep, they were up and away 'bright and early with that last day of term at school feeling'.[13] There had been no opportunity to send Headquarters a message about their imminent arrival so their approach to British lines was most cautious and once past the sentries, received a very warm welcome at Battalion HQ.

They soon heard that only one battalion, the Mahratta Light Infantry, had managed to cross the river but they had established a stronghold about one mile to the rear of Myaunglintha Village. The rest of the Brigade were to cross

13 Ibid.

shortly whereas the main drive was down the opposite bank of the river. They were greatly relieved to hand over their prisoners though they were on the receiving end of a lot of gentle teasing, 'A nice way to fight a war – going around with a couple of women.'[14]

With the British advance, it was obvious to the Burmese that the Japanese were fighting the remains of a losing battle and they started to take their revenge on their former oppressors. Lone Japanese soldiers, weakened by illness and starvation, were captured by villagers and executed; hideous torture often preceded their demise. Pro-Japanese villagers 'made themselves scarce'.[15] There was no shortage of volunteers to be Cecil's agents and 'information came pouring in. To sift this and determine how much was true and how much hearsay or sheer fabrication required hours of questioning. So many were the reports that we were receiving that I found I hadn't time to deal with them all myself so I arranged for Kya Twe and Thein Maung (who came from a police family and is now in the Police in Burma) to do the preliminary interrogation.'[16] Previously there was not enough intelligence coming in; now there was too much and it was an effort to encode it into a brief message with just the bare essentials.

Welfare air drops by Dakota enabled them to assist the villagers and to re-pay them for all their previous help. Bolts of cloth were dropped as clothing had been in very short supply during the Japanese occupation; white cotton parachute cloth was highly prized and parachute cords were un-wound and woven into clothes or used as fishing nets.

A message was received requesting Cecil's attendance at a Commando conference being held in Gwengu, so he set off on the seven-mile march and a mile short of the village he met an officer driving a jeep, running late because of the muddy tracks, having been asked 'to collect some amazing character who had been living behind the Jap lines for the last six weeks. I asked him if it was Major Merton by any chance and he said yes so I got in and drove back.'[17] After his introduction to the Commando company, Cecil was asked to open the proceedings, giving his views on the current situation. 'I had come firmly to the conclusion that delay in our advance down the East bank of the

14 Ibid.
15 Ibid.
16 Ibid.
17 Ibid.

Z Force bungalow. (Lieutenant General Sir Geoffrey Evans)

Chindwin might well prove fatal. That the Japs were at present weak on the ground but are reinforcing daily. They were ill-equipped but I had been told that it was their intention to repeat their old and, in the past, very successful tactics of allowing us to develop L of C [line of command] down the West bank of the Chindwin and then cut this, capturing our supply dumps for their own maintenance and so generally disrupting our main advance. I finished by saying that I thought this plan could easily be defeated if we smashed their small forces in the vicinity immediately.'[18] Cecil gave a detailed description of the Japanese camp near his intended air drop by the river, one that he had already asked to be bombed and finally it was, very successfully.

It was known that the Japanese had established a stronghold on a bend in the river but little information was known about the place. The Japanese

18 Ibid.

were using the villagers to provide materials but not allowing them into the stronghold area, so a bold agent taking advantage of the Japanese love of fish, devised a cunning approach. He started fishing well above the camp and slowly proceeded down the river. He attracted no attention at all until he was almost past the camp before a sentry challenged him, relieved him of his catch and sent him on his way. The agent's information was not very detailed but he gave an adequate description of the camp's layout.

The village was small with twenty or thirty bamboo huts on stilts built either side of a small track adjoining the main track. The Johnnies had slung their hammocks, tied to house posts halfway down the village under shade giving trees. Cecil awoke in the night to the tramp of boots approaching the village on the main track from the Mu river. Hurrying out of his hammock, he quickly woke the rest of the patrol, 'a heavily sleeping Burman isn't easy to rouse',[19] but shortly the footsteps faded away, to their great relief. They thought it was a Japanese patrol but were hugely relieved that they were not the enemy's objective. Cecil went straight to the Mahratta's post to get them to send a warning signal to HQ in Gwengu. As he followed the tracks up to the post, in total darkness guided by torchlight, he 'remembered wishing I had found out whether they are in the habit of setting booby traps on the track at night.'[20] Fortunately, they did not, but he found the post in a state of commotion as that morning a Mahratta fighting patrol had bumped into the Japanese at the river and had a brief, vicious fight resulting in a few casualties and killed some enemy soldiers including the officer. It transpired that the 'enemy patrol' heard in the small hours was the returning Mahrattas. 'The old Subedar Major, a fine soldier, who had led the patrol himself, would not let me leave until I had joined him in a slug of rum in celebration of this their first blood. Morale was extremely high and it boded well for the future'.[21]

With all his agents in place providing intelligence, Cecil decided that he was 'serving little useful purpose by remaining'[22] and he left for Mogaung where they had set off from 46 days previously. He spent a couple of days there disbanding his small force of villagers and writing testimonials for each

19 Ibid.
20 Ibid.
21 Ibid.
22 Ibid.

Z Force warriors. (Lieutenant General Sir Geoffrey Evans)

of them.[23] Finally, they crossed the river to the trucks waiting for them on the opposite bank and returned to Imphal on the now excellent motor road.

This proved to be his shortest patrol so far and he spent the next week being interviewed by various officers at HQ in Imphal; he felt that full use had not been made of the intelligence that he sent back during this patrol. When he was introduced to Major James Saunders, he announced that Cecil was 'a very angry officer'.[24] They became good friends and Cecil considered this Intelligence Officer to be very able; he was most saddened when Saunders was murdered several years later by bandits in Malaya where he had become a rubber planter.

23 A year later when Cecil was Chief Welfare Officer, he was on a tour accompanied by Minny and arrived at Schwegyin by station waggon. Whilst awaiting an LCT ferry on the banks of the Chindwin, a dugout canoe passed close to the shore. It was being paddled by a Burman who stared at them as he passed, gave a shout and paddled rapidly to the shore to greet Cecil. He was one of the faithful villagers and begged Cecil to visit the village again but sadly that was not possible at the time. From this man, Cecil learned that the ex-dacoit was pulled in by the police but Cecil's testimonial effected his release.

24 Ibid.

Cecil volunteered to command a patrol in the Karen Hills the following January which would be in advance of the Army, across the Irrawaddy. A new member of the Johnnies, Captain Willy Girsham was to be his second in command. A former Income Tax official in Burma who had been seconded to the Calcutta Income Tax Department after his evacuation from Burma in 1942. He had first been commissioned in the Great War and fought in Mesopotamia but was very fit, tough and considered his desk job far too sedentary. Cecil liked him instantly, 'I was delighted'[25] and the men of the patrol were most impressed too and they set off in Weapons Carriers for the Z Force training camp near Shillong, which had recently been established.

Cecil came down with another attack of malaria and was taken off to hospital and was 'imprisoned' there until he contrived an escape. He had a fever on admittance to hospital but had already been dosing himself with quinine so the fever soon passed but took advantage of a skin specialist's presence in the hospital to look at his Athletes Foot; a common problem in the jungle. This specialist, an Austrian, refused to allow Cecil to discharge himself despite pleading preparation for an important operation, although he was unable to disclose the nature of the operation. Knowing the order of the specialist's rounds, he arranged for the Z Force officers to have a truck waiting in the lane outside the hospital at 0900, visited the lavatory from where he could see the Brigadier's room next door to his and as soon as the specialist entered that room, he slipped out to the waiting truck with his packed haversack and sped off.

25 Ibid.

10

Maymyo

> "In peace there's nothing so becomes a man as modest stillness and humility: but when the blast of war blows in our ears, then imitate the action of the tiger."
>
> *Henry V* – William Shakespeare

Following Cecil's flight from hospital, he went straight to Calcutta and the ALFSEA Headquarters to make the final preparations for their ultimate patrol. A Karen uprising was timed to start when the army advance reached Pyinwara. Fearing the Johnnies' arrival would set this off prematurely, it was agreed that instead of the Karen Hills they would take a patrol to near Maymyo where the Japanese Army had their Headquarters and they investigated suitable gliding landing sites.

Before that, however, there was Christmas to celebrate in Calcutta with several other Z Force officers and 'a very good time was had by all'.[1]

News came through about the re-capture of Katha leaving Cecil on tenterhooks to receive information about Minny and the children who were last heard of in Katha. He was most excited on Boxing Day when the Brigadier General Staff (I) D A Prater, sent for Cecil and asked him if he would like to go and look for them. Of course, he jumped at the opportunity; Prater had fixed a Priority II Air Passage in Imphal for the following day and signalled the Army HQ to give him every assistance to get to Katha. 'I thought this was a magnificent gesture and much appreciated it.'[2]

1 Memoirs/papers of C G Merton IWM/05/11/1.
2 Ibid.

He flew to Imphal on Wednesday 27 December and the following day to Kawlin but was unable to continue to Katha much to his great disappointment but an American officer was waiting on the tarmac for a two-seater plane to collect and take him to Katha. He generously insisted on Cecil taking his place enabling him to get there after all. As soon as he got off the plane, a Burman rushed over to greet him. He had been the caretaker of the Government Rest House and knew Cecil and Minny well from their stays there. Immediately understanding why Cecil was there, he told him that on a trip to Mandalay six months earlier, he had heard that she was alive and well and in Aniskan. His note says '851 days since I saw Minny.'[3] His relief was immense but soon there were to be other worries. Wing Commander Forbes (known as 'No trouble at all' for his very cooperative manner) of Fourteenth Army HQ in Indainggale, knowing of Cecil's concerns, had sent ariel photographs showing that the house in Aniskan had received severe bomb damage. Further photographs were procured showing that the house had subsequently been completely destroyed. Now that Cecil knew his family had returned there, he was left worrying that they had been in the house when it was bombed, not knowing that the family had been thrown out of their home by the Commanding Officer of the Japanese air base at Aniskan.

On Friday 26 January 1945 a truck collected the Johnnies from the Calcutta Headquarters and drove them to Jessore Air strip for three days of parachute training. This was a Force 136[4] base and there were other groups present but no contact was allowed between the groups. It was here that Cecil was able to reveal the patrol's intended destination and, knowing the risks, made it clear that they could withdraw from it and be posted back to their regiments. He was most gratified that all were very positive and excited to be penetrating so deep behind Japanese lines and taking the fight to the enemy at last.

Gliders had finally been ruled out in favour of parachuting; parachuting-in had previously been considered non-operational for Z Force by every senior officer except Colonel Gregory. 'Even a small accident like a sprained ankle would mean that the victim would have to be left behind on his own to perish or be picked up and handed over to the Japanese which would have given away

3 Ibid.
4 The SOE (Special Operations Executive) in Burma.

the presence of the patrol. The only real alternative would be to shoot him and bury his body, something that nobody would want to contemplate'.[5]

They pored over maps and a huge mosaic of oblique aerial photographs to find the perfect Dropping Zone at Sinbyu Aing Lake (White Elephant Lake) as well as supply drops the other side of the Myitnge River. The country was covered in open scrub with widely spaced trees, none of which were over twenty feet high and would soon be shedding their leaves and with them, their cover. The gentle undulations on the Shan plateau were overlooked by the high hills beyond. The hills enabled a sight line for miles and because of this, it was agreed that the Dakota (and latterly fighters) supply drops must be at night. Hours were spent studying ariel photographs to familiarise themselves with the lake, the tributaries from the lake to the river, the rapids and suitable crossing places on the river (known crossings would be watched by the enemy).

Supplies of Christmas cake and a couple of bottles of rum fortified the patrol on their three-hour flight which set off from Jessore in the evening. Each man had a full water bottle in case they landed far from the Dropping Zone and could not reach their tributary by dawn. The rum 'kept up morale and I doubt if any of us ever seriously considered what could be in store for us. In fact, there was a sense of exhilaration that, after so many months on the borders between India and Burma this time we would be in the heart of Burma in the Mandalay area and very close to Japanese Army Headquarters in Maymyo.'[6] Through the open doors of the Dakota, they had spectacular views of the Shwebo Plain, the Irrawaddy River and the Shan Plateau. Cecil was able to look down, with bitter-sweet emotions, on the village of Aniskan. It was 877 days since he was last at home when he had three days leave in 1942. Co-incidentally, as Cecil was looking down onto Aniskan, Minny was in the garden assisting the friends who owned the hut she lived in. Their son was marrying the following day and the family were putting up decorations on large bamboo poles and were concerned that the poles might be mistaken for anti-aircraft guns. Minny recognised the plane as one which might be dropping British propaganda leaflets and planned to go and look for the leaflets; a courageous move on her part as just holding them could sign your death warrant. She had made a large collection of them which she had hidden, sewn inside her pillow; they gave her

5 Memoirs/papers of C G Merton IWM/05/11/1.
6 Ibid.

great hope and comfort. From these leaflets she knew of the British advance and the Japanese themselves bullishly informed her that British 'spies' were being parachuted into the area. A Burmese agent of the Japanese, a village Headman, called on her and said that Cecil might be dropped and offered to 'assist' her in his concealment. Knowing that he was a collaborator, she smiled, kept her silence and assured him that she would be in touch if Cecil should appear. From then on, she carried boiled eggs with her on her firewood collecting expeditions in case she found a ravenously hungry Cecil hiding in the forest.

At 2145, Cecil jumped in the first 'stick' with *Havildar* Kya Twe, Tai Cawn, Thein Maung and Thian Khaw Khai. Willy Girsham and the rest of the patrol were the second 'stick' followed by all their equipment. The high winds took them all off course and Cecil landed in a forest rather than the clearing he was aiming for. The drop had taken thirty minutes and all the equipment and men were found apart from Girsham, whom the patrol finally found having been knocked unconscious after hitting a tree, plummeting to the forest floor and landing on his spine. Months later it transpired that he had crushed his fifth and sixth vertebrae and fractured part of his pelvis but he never complained or let on what pain he was in for the duration of the patrol.

Dropped in the wrong position, they skirted villages and headed down to the river, desperate to find the correct tributary. Completely exhausted but fearful of falling asleep, Cecil used his Everest rucksack's aluminium frame as a back rest whilst he lay on the forest floor but, if he fell asleep, his head would hit the frame and wake him up again. They could only afford a short rest before moving off but hunger forced them to stop again and cook their meal whilst the wireless was rigged up. The dawn light allowed them to use the code card and encipher a short message to report their safe landing.

As soon as they finished their transmission, they heard the sounds of men coming up the stream towards them. A line of thirty or forty men, some in khaki with rifles and others obviously villagers in *longyis* (sarongs) with towels wrapped around their heads. The patrol hid amongst the rocks prepared 'to sell our lives as dearly as possible. I couldn't help thinking that my message to army had been a little premature.'[7] The party of men stopped short of the hidden patrol and headed up the right bank and into the distance whilst the Johnnies

7 Ibid.

Cecil's patrol air dropped south-west of Maymyo in January 1945. Back row: second from left Cecil Merton; third from left Havildar Kya Twe; fourth Willy Girsham, fifth Tun Nyunt. Front row: third from left Tai Cawn. (Lieutenant General Sir Geoffrey Evans)

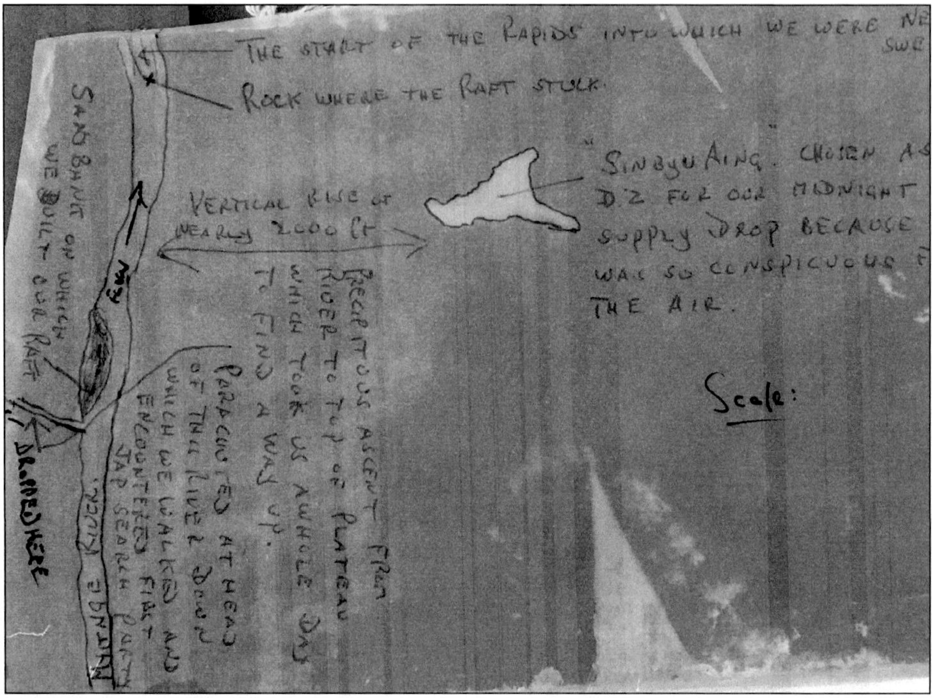

Hand-drawn map of Sinbyu Aing Lake. (IWM/05/11/1)

remained 'frozen' in their hiding places until the possibility of any stragglers had passed. A short distance ahead was an old man with his small granddaughter, searching the rock pools for shrimps and she was heading towards the hiding soldiers. A scream from her might well alert the search party in the distance. Thein Maung, the only Burman in the patrol, swiftly removed his uniform, changed into his *longyi* and he casually walked towards the girl and her grandfather to find out the name of this stream; the name did not tally with their supposed position, although often a river would have many different local names. Thein Maung often used the cover of an opium smuggler in these circumstances, making him most welcome in the area as opium smoking was rife, and no one would question if he was wary or nervous in that line of business.

After that, their progress along the river bed was straightforward heading for the Myitgne River and their crossing, as well as the planned supply drop. The small supply of rations that they were carrying were not to everyone's taste

– dehydrated beetroot being a major part of it. Carrying a photograph of the river crossing, they were relieved to finally reach their destination and started building a raft, hoping to be across the river before dark. A lack of suitable large bamboo meant they eventually used large logs on the side of the river but the raft was not completed until midnight. The two strongest swimmers, Tai Cawn and Tun Nyunt were to swim to the other side with ropes made from twisted parachute cord and pull the raft with all the equipment on it. The rest of the men, stripped to their underpants, swam alongside and pushed the raft as hard as they could. The overpowering current, a hidden rock and the weakness of the cord rope all combined to cause disaster just five yards from the far bank so the men hurriedly threw their equipment from the raft to the bank. Unable to lift the waterlogged rucksacks, the men formed a chain to pass vital equipment like the wireless and rucksacks to the bank and succeeded in doing so before the raft broke up and tumbled down the rapids. A little bit of water had seeped into the wireless which needed to be left open in the air to dry and the men were freezing in the windy gorge in their sodden underwear. It was far too dangerous to light a big, blazing fire there but the cold could bring out the malaria that they all carried in their blood, so they risked a small fire, hung their clothes on strung up washing lines and cooked a substantial meal with a brew-up. Before dawn they were ready to move off again but struggled to find a pathway up the steep sides of the gorge and its overhanging rocks. It was decided that two men, without packs, should climb ahead to find a route and Cecil and Kya Twe finally scrambled over the top after a two hour climb to the wonderful sight of Sinbyu Aing Lake, their planned drop zone. This lake, named for white elephants, was considered to have magical properties by the superstitious Shan people. It was able to dispel all your worries and was a refuge to people in distress; it certainly was to the Johnnies at this time. Once all the men had climbed up by midday, the lake had worked its magic on all of them. A firewood collection allowed them to build another fire to continue drying out the wireless and a flare path was laid for the supply drop. A final meal of dehydrated rations whilst they imagined all the luxuries that would soon be dropped for them from above; all had had enough of dehydrated beetroot. So much in fact that Cecil was concerned he had damaged his kidneys in the river crossing and was producing blood in his urine before realising that it was the preponderance of beetroot. At midnight the Dakota roared overhead and the drop went without a hitch; the next three days were spent hiding the parachutes and finding safe food dumps under boulders and in crevices. A lack of army biscuits – there were always biscuits – meant that one parachute was missing and they searched high and low for it but later found out that the loss was a blessing in disguise. It had dropped ten miles away and was found by some farmers who took it to their fields. A Japanese search party assumed that they were in contact with the Johnnies and when the farmers were unable to give them any information they were badly beaten up. The Japanese switched their search to that area giving the Johnnies a few day's peace and quiet.

Great emphasis had been made at Army headquarters to discover the location of the wireless transmitter of the Japanese Army headquarters in Maymyo. The ariels had not been spotted in the jungle by air reconnaissance so the Johnnies moved to the village of Pyingyi, which was nearest to their hide out and studied the villagers, at dawn, through binoculars. Thein Maung donned his usual disguise as an opium smuggler and sauntered into the village, asked for the Headman and offered him a supply of opium. Leading the Headman out of the village towards his 'supply', the Headman saw the uniforms of the Johnnies and turned to flee before being rugby tackled by Tun Nyunt. His first words were 'You must be the parachutists dropped in at Kyawku.' Asked how he had heard of them, he said he had heard about them in Maymyo from the Japanese. He had to produce labour gangs repairing the railway yards there and had been asked to keep a look out and to report the parachutists. An intelligent, reliable, strict Buddhist who had been appointed Headman by the British Government, U Aung Sint was fiercely pro-British; he and Cecil took to each other immediately. He was able to tell Cecil that the ariels were twelve miles away amongst Pagodas at a Buddhist monastery; the monks had been evicted and it was now guarded by a detachment of Japanese soldiers.

The Johnnies felt very pleased with themselves but their positivity was short lived when they met U Aung Sint the following day and he nervously told them that the previous evening thirty Japanese soldiers commanded by a Sergeant, had marched into the village and requestioned some houses whilst they searched the area for the parachutists who had been dropped near Kyawku. It was a blow to learn that the Japanese were searching for them in that area; hoping that they would concentrate on the drop area. Cecil never discovered if they had been spotted on arrival or subsequently betrayed by traitorous villagers or the Japanese had just assumed that the parachutists would make for the Maymyo area. From now on it was a matter of leaving no trace of their presence in the area, marching slowly and cautiously in single file and the last man erasing all footprints. Never leaving cigarette butts, cellophane wrappings, lavatory paper or anything that the villagers would or could not use. Even cigarette ash had to be hidden under rocks as the locals all smoked homemade bamboo pipes or cheroots rolled from local tobacco. Camps were made at the water's edge and immediately after cooking the stones were put into deep water and ashes were washed downstream. Anything buried had to be deep enough not to be dug up by wild animals.

Cecil received a message from Headquarters stating, 'Do not attempt to contact your wife as she is being watched.' On the one hand, that message was uplifting as it proved she was still alive but on the other, it gave rise to countless more fears. Thein Maung offered to go to Aniskan to find out where she was, but Cecil would not consider putting him in such danger. Cecil never discovered the source of this information.

A rendezvous with U Aung Sint produced much more information including the Japanese discovery of the lost supply parachute and the beatings of the farmers who found it. The search parties went out every morning from the village and returned each evening to sleep there, giving the patrol peace of mind that they were safe in the hours of darkness. At the next meeting, the Headman told them that the search parties were out looking for them in the lake area and not to return there (apart from at night when the Japanese were asleep in the village to gather the contents of their supply dumps). This meant that they had to find a new camp, close enough to water and not too far from Pyingyi and their intelligence source. After a day of searching, they found a narrow stream with twenty-foot bamboo growing out of the low, flat banks. This gave them shade, cover and though the *chaung* was not flowing, recent rains had filled a rock pool giving them a water source providing at least a months' worth of cooking water. A supply drop gave them some unheard of luxuries like fresh bread, rum and New Zealand lamb chops which were so appreciated after days of dehydrated rations. The Canadian Squadron based at Tully Hall airstrip near Imphal took great care of the patrol and their welfare; they even managed to get Senior Service cigarettes rather than the 'notorious' V brand and put several packets into the drops. Understanding the patrol's situation, they flew wide swoops to divert enemy attention as well as very low at personal risk to themselves. Sometimes so low that the parachutes did not have time to open and the containers just dropped to the ground. These were fighters rather than Dakotas and the Japanese never suspected that fighters might be dropping supplies and would dive for cover at the sight of low flying fighters – all part of the subterfuge.

Meetings with the Headman were every five days giving him or his son time to get into Maymyo and in between meetings they were lying low in their hide out, hunted all the while. They listened to All India Radio every morning at 0800 and heard the news that 19th Division were on the outskirts of Madaya, twenty miles north of Mandalay. They expected Maymyo and Mandalay to be taken any day without realising that the heavy, early rains which had filled their rock pool, had prevented tanks heading south and so the advance had been halted for several weeks. The toll of a double life; reporting to the Johnnies whilst the Japanese lived in his village, was taking a toll on U Aung Sint. He looked haggard, nervous and exhausted with a bad eye infection and Cecil offered to get medicine for his eyes in the next supply drop.

The next drop was on 7 March and these were a time of great nerves. However low the planes managed to fly, the sight of parachutes descending was visible for miles if being waited and watched for. The 'chutes were a myriad of colours; red and blue, green and orange and other different combinations, all made of pure silk and designed to be as conspicuous as possible; the Johnnies wished it were the opposite.

The advance south had resumed and there was fighting on the outskirts of Mandalay and other forces had crossed the Irrawaddy and were closing in from the West. This news cheered up both the Johnnies and U Aung Sint hugely. His eye infection had cleared up and he was much happier though the Japanese in his village were not; they could not understand how the 'parachutists' had evaded capture for all this time. In their frustration, they had started threatening and accusing the villagers and were sending them out searching for footprints. U Aung Sint begged The Johnnies to get as far away as possible for their own good. Cecil felt that, if it were not for the good news from the front, he would have taken the advice of the Headman and left. They had been in the area for five weeks now, evading capture daily and the forest fires which were rife at this time of the year, left a carpet of ash in which footprints could not be hidden. 'It was though the period of most intense nervous tension that we had ever been through throughout our career in Z Force. In all our other patrols there was the knowledge that at any moment something disastrous could happen but this was something rather remote and would probably never happen. Now we had the feeling that disaster was imminent and that it was only a question of days, hours or perhaps only minutes before it struck.'[8]

The news on All India Radio was more positive every day and a message was waiting for them 'You are safe when you reach Flagstaff House.' This was a big house on top of a hill in the outskirts of Maymyo, used by the Commander in Chief of the Armed Forces when Maymyo was in use as the summer capital of Burma. This cryptic message meant that Maymyo had been re-captured and therefore Mandalay must have fallen too. They had their routine meeting with a hugely relieved U Aung Sint who had heard the news too. One hundred Japanese had arrived in his village on their way to Taunggyi, demanding guides and boats to cross the river.

Morale had been boosted; 'after all the tension we had been under we now almost had the feeling that the war was over.'[9] Cecil could hardly contain his impatience to go and search for his family but they still had a job to do; watching the Japanese withdrawal and alerting the air force who were harassing the retreating enemy. The Japanese were pouring through Pyingyi, stopping for the night and discussing their routes with U Aung Sint and departing the following morning with guides organised by the Headman, before he came to tell Cecil the numbers, rank, identification and route directions of these soldiers. Cecil would then encode a message passing on all this information and recommendations of where to strafe them en route.

Once the Japanese exodus was no longer pouring through the area, the patrol felt they were safe to go into Maymyo, before first arranging with U Aung Sint to help collect their stores from the lake area. Once the villagers had returned the Headman's son told Cecil that they were amazed to know where the patrol had been hiding as that was where the Japanese had concentrated their searches. Every known water source had been thoroughly searched by the Japanese so they chose well in their second hiding place with the unpredicted water supply in the *chaung*.

Finally, after fifty-three days of playing their potentially lethal game of cat-and-mouse, they set off from Pyingyi on 21 March, in high spirits. 'I say light hearts but for myself also with trepidation. All this time I had been buoying myself up with belief that I would find my family safe. I knew that I had no reason

8 Ibid.
9 Ibid.

to believe this but I also knew that I just could not afford to allow myself to think otherwise. I knew how heavily the odds were against them. We had all heard tales of Japanese atrocities and their treatment of women. Even if they survived all that how were they able to live. We heard how rice, which cost fifteen rupees a bag before the war now cost two thousand and all other commodities had risen likewise. Webby had left her a couple of thousand rupees but that was the price of a bag of rice which would last them about a month. She had her jewellery which would bring her in quite a bit but had she been able to keep this with all the looting and dacoity that had taken place. Even if she had kept it it would not have been sufficient to support her all this time. The house I knew had been destroyed and presumably with all its contents. No, really, I had no reason for optimism if it was optimism. Really it was a matter of refusing to face facts. Now this would be avoided no longer; soon I would know the truth one way or another.'[10]

On the forest track winding down the Sa Byaik Chaung Valley, they encountered a nervous woman carrying vegetables who informed them that soldiers were coming. On asking if she meant Japanese soldiers, she replied that they were American and round the next corner, they ran into a column of thirty or forty men wearing peaked caps similar to the Japanese or Chinese armies. A short, terrifying stand-off was soon elevated to relief when the Kachin *Subedar*, formerly of the Burma Rifles but now seconded to the American Strategic Services, stepped forward and introduced himself. Cecil's fear of being the victims of 'friendly fire' nearly came to pass at this eleventh hour.

Their route took them into Inya village where a group of Anglo-Burmese, disguised as Burmese throughout the occupation, greeted them with the most tremendous welcome and insisted that they share what little food they had in celebration. Asking if anyone knew of his wife, one replied that they had heard of a Mrs Martin, wife of an Englishman living in Aniskan near the railway station. As excited as Cecil was, he could not decline the honour of the 'banquet' being given for them and asking if there was a bicycle that he could borrow, set off as soon as he could leaving Girsham and the rest of the patrol in Inya. He pedalled for thirty minutes through the jungle to the outskirts of Maymyo, full expecting to be held up at any moment by some trigger-happy soldier. The neat, painted bungalows of the Maymyo of his memory were gone and in their place were roofless, dilapidated, empty houses overtaken by the bush and he hardly knew where

10 Ibid.

he was but followed the main road into the town centre and finally out on the road to Aniskan. He reached the station where he was told the family lived and met a Burman who recognised Cecil immediately. He offered to guide Cecil to the two-storey house belonging to U Pye and left Cecil in the garden from where he could see a small bamboo hut and two girls and a boy playing. 'Surely the biggest was my daughter June and the other little girl would be about the age of my youngest daughter Fiona … I called out 'Are you June?' The children looked around startled and prepared to run. The villager, who unnoticed by me had remained standing by the gate shouted in Burmese 'This is your father.' As the children stood hesitantly somebody looked out of the hut. The guide called out 'The *Thakin* (Master) has come back.' My wife heard this and came dashing out, looked, saw me and rushed to greet me and so ended 1087 days of separation and suspense wondering if we would ever find each other alive again. To Fiona I was a stranger and even June was a little shy of the father she had not seen for three years.'[11]

Once Minny had control of her emotions she pulled Cecil into the security of the hut as only that morning ten Japanese soldiers had come to the house demanding food. She told him of the family's close escape with the *Kampeitai* truck's ambush and that there were still Japanese soldiers in Maymyo, ironically at Flagstaff House which Cecil had been informed was secure. Distant gun fire could be heard from the direction of Mandalay which reminded him that 'though my private war may now be over, the other one was far from finished.'[12] Cecil retired that night, happy but anxious, to an actual bed (bamboo platform with a grass sleeping mat, pillows and a blanket) after so many nights in the open and noticed a long Burmese sword by the bed. Minny had kept it there in case any Japanese should try and molest her in the night, telling Cecil that she would not have hesitated to use it and then to turn it on herself afterwards.

'I suppose that must have been one of the happiest periods of my life finding myself once more united with my family and they [are] all unscathed by the war. It is in circumstances such as these that one really appreciates the true values in life. I now had absolutely everything I wanted in life and the fact that our house and all our belongings had gone meant absolutely nothing. I could just relax in the warming atmosphere of my own home amongst the greetings of our friends. I have no doubt that all soldiers home on leave from the front

11 Ibid.
12 Ibid.

must have experienced this but how much more so in my case when I never knew whether 'home' existed any longer and knew that the odds were very, very much against it. The day passed in a feeling of bliss.'[13]

Willy Girsham and the patrol arrived later and they were billeted in a large house by the railway line and though empty of furniture, provided a smooth floor and a roof over their heads for the first time in months. A supply drop was made the following morning and about one hundred neighbours and friends came to watch in fiesta mood – 'quite the happiest event for the past three years and was celebrated as such. The ladies donned their brightest *longyis* and best white muslin jackets which they had stored away for use only on Pagoda festivals and other such festive occasions. Many were carrying dainty coloured parasols. The men were wearing their best *pasoes* [pasose or paso – a sheet of cloth folded to look like trousers] and neat jackets with bright coloured silk handkerchiefs. It was the typical scene at an important Pagoda festival'.[14] Unlike the furtive, night-time drops, this was in full day-light with a party atmosphere and the pilots made extra, low level sweeps over the festival scene.

The final mission was complete and arrangements were made for the patrol's withdrawal to India in mid-April but Cecil requested War Leave to be spent in Aniskan, which was soon granted. Rest and recuperation were the order of the day. Japanese stragglers were still passing through so the safest place was home. A message was sent to U Aung Sint who arrived by bullock cart with the patrol's equipment and stores and a happy reunion was held with him. He held them all in awe, an almost 'supernatural respect' as he could not fathom how they had managed to evade the Japanese search parties. Jungle villagers are most superstitious and he put their survival down to the legend of Sinbyu Aing Lake as well as their own supernatural abilities. Forest fires had burnt out all the dried grass and bamboo around their supply dump but not the contents and this added to his superstitions of divine protection. They made a presentation of large quantities of coloured parachute silk and arranged an official award from the Burma Government for his assistance and bravery.

The shotgun and rifle cartridges had arrived in the bullock cart and Kya Twe set off with it to shoot a barking deer for the pot. He did not return at lunchtime as expected and, by nightfall, they were worried about his absence. At dawn an

13 Ibid.
14 Ibid.

excitable villager appeared with the news that a long column of Japanese soldiers with pack mules had marched along the track through his village, passing straight by the house where the patrol was sleeping, over the railway line, onto the Mandalay-Maymyo road and eastwards towards the Myitnge River. Kya Twe suddenly appeared mid-morning and told how he, dressed in nothing but a *longyi* and carrying the shotgun, had been surrounded and captured by the column. Ordered to guide the soldiers to the next village, he could not admit that he did not know the country (being a Karen) and he chose what he hoped was the correct track to the next village and the humane commander released him at the end; often guides were immediately bumped off, to use Cecil's turn of phrase.

In Pegu, following the Japanese surrender, Cecil met a Brigade Intelligence Officer who told him that when they captured the Japanese Headquarters there, they found a copy of a notice stating, 'Major Merton had been dropped in with a party of men' and called on all villagers to report any signs of their presence and the offer of an award for their capture, dead or alive. 'We felt quite pleased with ourselves that the Japs believed that we only penetrated their lines by being parachuted in'[15] little realising that they had marched into occupied country again and again.

Twenty-six Johnnie patrols had taken place over three and a half years culminating in the defeat of Japan. They were awarded: one CBE, two DSOs, four OBEs, four MBEs, seventeen MCs (two bars) and sixteen Burma Gallantry Awards. Cecil lists awards given to his patrol and those that assisted them:

I. Military Medal

a) Kya Twe (leader of party since August 1942)
b) Tun Nyunt (with party since August 1942. Has been most reliable man)

II. British Empire Medal

a) Ko Khai (with party since May 1944. Very good man)
b) Thein Pe (with party since August 1942)
c) Goulman Lama (with party since August 1942)
d) Tai Cawn (with party since August 1942)
e) Dum Hpaw Gam (with party since August 1942 but captured in October 1943)

15 Ibid.

III. Civil Decoration equivalent to MM

a) Maung Thein Maung (the only civilian in the party and as such is not eligible for the MM but has done the most distinguished work and made contacts etc in civil dress)

IV. D B B L Gun Certificate

a) U Aung Sint – Headman Pyingyi Village, Maymyo subdivision (assisted in every way on Maymyo patrol. He warned us of the direction in which Japs were beating for us and enabled us to dodge them. Collected information for us)
b) Hpaula Sao Gam – Headman Hpaola Village, Lonton Township, Myitkyina Division

V. DAH Certificate

a) Maung Ba Thike – son of U Po Tha, Mogaung Village, Paungbyin Township, Upper Chindwin (acted as Headman to my porters on my Oil Indaw patrol. Went into villages and made contacts for me)

VI. Certificate

a) Maung Ba Hlaing – son of U Shwe Kun, Mogaung Village (all below acted as ports on my Oil Indaw patrol and were with us 2 months in trying conditions)
b) Maung Kyaw Pwint – son of U San Lon, Inbauk Village
c) Maung Po Onn – son of Po Yan Shin, Mogaung Village
d) Maung Ohn Pe – son of Po Tha Haung, Thazi Village
e) Maung Kyan – of Mogaung Village

VII. ATM (Burmese Government Civil Award)

a) Van Kio – Chief Shurkhua Village, Chin Hills (rendered very valuable resistance when in his area where my HQ was for 3 months)
b) Lam Ko Thang – Chief Dolluang Village, Chin Hills (rendered very valuable assistance in Kalemyo area. Accompanied us on patrol)[16]

16 Ibid.

Anglo-Burman Jimmy Middleton, a former official of the Bombay Burma Trading Corporation, was the only member of the Johnnies killed in action by a mortar bomb blast in the Kabaw Valley in 1943, although there were many close shaves. His partner George 'Red' Parker observed, 'In Middleton, Z Force lost a very gallant officer and gentleman and I, a very good friend'[17]

In a letter to Colonel Shelley in November 1945, Brigadier General Staff (I). D A Prater wrote:

> *Dear Shelley*
> *Many thanks for your letter of 31 October. The day of our parting with Z Force was a sad one for Intelligence here and I would like to mark it by expressing our deep appreciation (in which I know I speak for all Intelligence Officers in our formations) of the valuable work your Force achieved.*
>
> *Z Force, I have no hesitation in saying, remained the best single source of tactical intelligence in Burma; and in the form you had reorganised it for Malaya would I am convinced have done us equally sterling work.*
>
> *We all of us send to you and your men, our best wishes for the future, and again our thanks for a job well done.*
>
> *Yours sincerely*[18]

Cecil was awarded his first MC gazetted on 16 August 1945 and the bar to it on 17 January 1946. The Citation reads:

> *Patrolled during the campaigning seasons of 1942–43 and 1943–44 on the Chindwin Front in advance of our forward troops, first as Second-in-Command of Major Parry's patrol, and later as a patrol leader. In the latter part of the campaigning season of 1943–44, he led a special patrol on Special Force Front. Carried out numerous daring and dangerous reconnaissance's, had a number of clashes with the enemy, and produced much valuable information. Has shown the most consistent gallantry, and a complete disregard for his own safety. One of the finest Patrol Leaders in Z Force.*
>
> *Recommended by Colonel J P Shelley, Commander Z Force and countersigned by Director of Intelligence, India Command and recommended by Lt Gen, C-in-C Allied Land Forces South East Asia.*

17 Ibid.
18 Ibid.

The second citation read:

> *Major Merton led a recce patrol in the Chaung Zauk area east of the Chindwin during Oct and Nov 1944. In Jan 45 he again volunteered to lead a patrol. He undertook a parachute course and he and his patrol were dropped into the area East of Maymyo on 26 Jan 1945. Unfortunately, the patrol was dropped into the wrong area, during a high wind and from a great height. The party landed on a rugged hilltop and many of them were hung up in high trees. Major Merton displayed extreme courage and leadership. He worked throughout the night and the following day in extricating his men and rallying the patrol who were dispersed over a large area. He then led them towards Maymyo across the Mytinge River at a most dangerous point, where there were rapids. An improvised raft was constructed and the patrol only narrowly escaped drowning when this sank. Shortly after the crossing the patrol was given away to the enemy, who pursued the patrol for over a fortnight. Major Merton again displayed a very high standard of leadership and with a total disregard for his own safety produced some extremely valuable intelligence.*
>
> *Recommended by Brigadier J S Lethbridge, Brigadier General Staff, HQ Fourteenth Army; recommended by Lieutenant-General W J Slim GOC-in-Chief, Fourteenth Army and signed by him again as General, C-in-C Allied Land Forces South East Asia.*[19]

19 Cecil's medals were sold by auction at Spinks on 25 November 2010 for the hammer price of £15,000 (£18,000 including premium). Spink & Co. website states, 'he was one of the finest patrol leaders in Z Force' and the website's author's 'favourite' medals set.

11

Horizons

> "A symbol of British ruggedness"
> James Lunt about Cecil

A return to peace, family life and happiness was topped with the birth of Zienia at the beginning of December 1945. Named for Z Force, her birth completed the family unit and sealed the peace in Burma for the Merton family. Cecil retained his temporary rank of Major on the South East Asia list. In November 1945 he became a S O II, H2 and Civil Affairs staff officer.

Cecil relinquished his commission on 18 May 1946 (gazetted 22 April 1946), leaving the army with the honorary rank of Major. He started working for the Rehabilitation Department of the Burmese Government as Chief Evacuee Welfare Officer. He commenced the job on 1 January 1946 on the salary of R1,350[1] plus £30[2] overseas pay but 'the interminable delay about finance has evidently blunted the edge of his keenness and it looks as if we are going to lose a really good man'[3] wrote a Government Secretary as Cecil resigned due to the shortage of funding in the department. He re-joined his old firm Messrs Foucar & Co Ltd and was appointed Circle Manager, Upper Burma and in 1947 he became the General Forest Manager in charge of all the Forest Leases based out of Rangoon.

Foucar's General Manager, C G B Scovell writes in a letter of recommendation in 1949 that 'Mr Merton is a man of the highest character and is absolutely

1 Equivalent to £4,273 in 2020.
2 Equivalent to £1,305 in 2020.
3 Letter from Additional Secretary and Director 3.7.1946, Memoirs/papers of C G Merton IWM/05/11/1.

reliable in every way. He is hardworking, has plenty of drive and initiative, and does not fear responsibility. He is physically active, has generally had very good health, and has great powers of endurance. He has always shown great keenness in his work and had managed his areas with efficiency and success. When, on the liberation of Burma, I had to get staff together to reopen the Company's activities, he was one of the first for whom I asked; and I was very glad when he decided to give up his welfare job and rejoin Foucars.'[4]

When Burma gained its independence on 4 January 1948, the forests were nationalised and Cecil became a Zone Manager in the State Timber Extraction Organisation. After Independence life got more and more difficult for 'foreigners' in Burma and in 1950 the family moved to Singapore where Cecil started working for Montague Meyer,[5] a large timber enterprise still in existence today. Then to Sarawak where he worked for Liddell Bros & Co. in first Seriki and then Sibu in the Second Division of Sarawak.[6]

In 1960 the family moved to Britain where together they ran a boarding house in Willesden Green for Burmese and Thai students whilst he worked for the United Nations Food and Agriculture Organisation[7] which involved much travelling. They were not happy in Britain and wanted to return to the Far East and he secured a post as Conservator of Forests in Brunei. He was well known and much admired throughout British North Borneo. When his nephew Lieutenant-Colonel Robin Merton, son of Walter,[8] served in Kuching in the early 1960s, he met many expatriates who knew the family well and thought very highly of Cecil.

In 1968, he retired from the Brunei Forestry Service and through the offices of Sir Denis White, the British High Commissioner in Brunei, was appointed Controller of the Sultan of Brunei's Household in London. Cecil and Minny were contented living in London with all three of their daughters grown up and independent, so it came as a tremendous shock when Cecil died of a heart attack on 26 October 1969 at the relatively young age of 61.[9] He was buried in

4 C G B Scovell, General Manager of Foucar & Co. Ltd, Rangoon letter of recommendation, 30.4.1949, Memoirs/papers of C G Merton IWM/05/11/1.

5 Founded in 1906 by Montague L Meyer.

6 Sarawak came under the domain of the Sultan of Brunei.

7 Founded in 1945 to raise levels of nutrition, improve the lives of rural peoples and increase agricultural productivity. Their motto is: *Fiat Panis* – Let there be bread.

8 Air Chief Marshal Sir Walter Hugh Merton GBE, KCB, OBE.

9 Probate states that he left £19,200 – equivalent to £336,132 in 2020.

Hampstead Cemetery leaving Minny to mourn during a long, lonely widowhood until she joined him in 2005. To survive all that he had survived in those dark, belligerent days only to drop dead on the streets of a post-bellum London is cruelly ironic; 'Merton, four-square, a symbol of British ruggedness'[10] who was 'one of the finest Patrol Leaders in Z Force'.

We are not afraid of anything!
We are daring and brave
Ready to sacrifice our lives
With Parpahein marching to the royal city
On this day fixed as the day of victory.

At our camp in the forest
Verdant are the branches
Full of small flower buds;
Sweet are the sounds
Of the military drums and gongs
In the soft evening's twilight.

Just as mists and clouds are dispersed
So too must we destroy our enemy
The elder brother Zeyathein

U Kyin U (c.1773 – Sinbaungwe, Magway Region)

'We were Fourteenth Army, the final echo of Kipling's world, the very last British soldiers in the old imperial tradition. I don't say we were happy to be in Burma, because we weren't, but we knew that Slim was right when he said 'Someday, you'll be proud to say, 'I was there'.[11]

10 Lunt, James, *The Retreat from Burma 1941-1942* (London: David & Charles Publishers, 1986), p.180.
11 McDonald Fraser, George, *Safely Quartered Out Here* (London: Harper Collins, 1992).

Numb. 37223 4157

SUPPLEMENT
TO
The London Gazette

Of TUESDAY, the 14th of AUGUST, 1945

Published by Authority

Registered as a newspaper

THURSDAY, 16 AUGUST, 1945

CENTRAL CHANCERY OF THE ORDERS OF KNIGHTHOOD.

St. James's Palace, S.W.1,
16th August, 1945.

The KING has been graciously pleased to give orders for the following promotion in, and appointments to the Most Excellent Order of the British Empire, in recognition of gallant and distinguished services in the field:—

To be an Additional Commander of the Military Division of the said Most Excellent Order:—

Colonel (temporary) John Patrick SHELLEY, O.B.E. (761), Grenadier Guards (ret. pay).

To be an Additional Officer of the Military Division of the said Most Excellent Order:—

Lieutenant-Colonel (temporary) Charles Eric Cyril GREGORY (862), 18th Royal Garhwal Rifles, Indian Army.

To be an Additional Member of the Military Division of the said Most Excellent Order:—

Captain (temporary) Thomas Arthur MENDES (4384), Intelligence Corps, Indian Army.

CENTRAL CHANCERY OF THE ORDERS OF KNIGHTHOOD.

St. James's Palace, S.W.1,
16th August, 1945.

The KING has been graciously pleased to approve the award of the British Empire Medal (Military Division), in recognition of gallant and distinguished services in the field, to the undermentioned:—

No. 5048054 Private Geoffrey AITKEN, The North Staffordshire Regiment (The Prince of Wales's).
No. 6137573 Colour-Sergeant John William BEACH, The East Surrey Regiment.

ERRATA.

The Appointment of Major-General (temporary) Leslie Burtonshaw NICHOLLS, C.B.E. (8826), late Royal Corps of Signals, to be an Additional Member of the Military Division of the Third Class, or Companions, of the Most Honourable Order of the Bath, which was published in the London Gazette (No. 37204) dated 2nd August, 1945, is cancelled; this officer having been appointed to be an Additional Member of the Military Division of the Third Class, or Companions, of the said Most Honourable Order in the London Gazette (No. 37138) dated 21st June, 1945.

War Office, 16th August, 1945.

The KING has been graciously pleased to approve the following awards in recognition of gallant and distinguished services in the field:—

The Distinguished Service Order.

Major (temporary) Samuel NEWLAND (5592), Intelligence Corps, Indian Army.

The Military Cross.

Major (temporary) Cecil Gerald MERTON (189643), General List.
Major (temporary) George Edgar PARKER, M.B.E. (9368), 6th Rajputana Rifles, Indian Army.
Major (temporary) John Keith PARRY (5386), 6th Rajputana Rifles, Indian Army.
Major (temporary) William Archibald GOLDBERG (5850), Intelligence Corps, Indian Army.
Major (temporary) Dennis Wilmot RAE (9652), General List, Indian Army.
Major (temporary) Richard Wiloughby WOOD (ABRO.76), Army in Burma Reserve of Officers.
Major (temporary) Zaw Gawng (ABRO.946), Army in Burma Reserve of Officers.

War Office, 16th August, 1945.

The KING has been graciously pleased to approve that the following be Mentioned in recognition of gallant and distinguished services in the field:—

INDIAN ARMY.

INFANTRY.

15 Punjab R.

Capt. (temp.) J. G. MIDDLETON (4421) (killed in action).

War Office, 16th August, 1945.

The KING has been graciously pleased to approve the following awards in recognition of gallant and distinguished services in North West Europe:—

Bar to the Distinguished Service Order.

Lieutenant-Colonel (temporary) Iain Arthur MURRAY, D.S.O. (99246), Glider Pilot Regiment, Army Air Corps.

The Distinguished Flying Cross.

Captain (temporary) Raymond George COLES (233903), Royal Regiment of Artillery (Highgate).
Major (temporary) Burton Henry JACKSON (95473), The East Surrey Regiment (attached Glider Pilot Regiment, Army Air Corps) (Cirencester).

Gazette 14.8.45. (*The London Gazette*)

498 SUPPLEMENT TO THE LONDON GAZETTE, 17 JANUARY, 1946

No. 37262, dated the 13th September, 1945:—

Page 4557:
For No. S/106608 Staff-Sergeant William Lindsay MEARNS, Royal Army Service Corps.
Read No. S/106608 Staff-Sergeant Walter Lindsay MEARNS, Royal Army Service Corps.

No. 37274, dated the 20th September, 1945:—

Page 4674:
For No. 553443 Staff Quarter-Master-Sergeant Arthur John RICHARDSON-GEORGE, Royal Corps of Signals.
Read No. 553443 Squadron Quarter-Master-Sergeant Arthur John RICHARDSON-GEORGE, Royal Corps of Signals.

Page 4674:
For No. S/10690310 Warrant Officer Class II (acting) Alexander Walter SMITH, Royal Army Service Corps.
Read No. S/10690310 Warrant Officer Class II (acting) Alexander Walker SMITH, Royal Army Service Corps.

Page 4674:
For No. SR.599256V Sergeant Dimitri Constan TATOS, South African Forces.
Read No. SR.599256V Sergeant Constan Demetri TATOS, South African Forces.

No. 37302, dated the 11th October, 1945:—

Page 4996:
For No. S/135962 Sergeant Aaron FREEMAN, Royal Army Service Corps.
Read No. S/135962 Sergeant Aaron FREEDMAN, Royal Army Service Corps.

Page 4996:
For No. 2568372 Staff Quarter-Master-Sergeant (acting) Andrew Cameron YOUNG, Royal Corps of Signals.
Read No. 2568372 Squadron Quarter-Master-Sergeant (acting) Andrew Cameron YOUNG, Royal Corps of Signals.

No. 37310, dated the 18th October, 1945:—

Page 5097:
For No. 7258996 Staff-Sergeant James HALLEY, Royal Armoured Corps.
Read No. 7258996 Staff-Sergeant James HALLEY, Royal Army Medical Corps.

War Office, 17th January, 1946.

The KING has been graciously pleased to approve the following awards in recognition of gallant and distinguished services in Burma:—

Bar to the Distinguished Service Order.

Brigadier (acting) Lewis Henry Owain PUGH, D.S.O. (37091), Royal Regiment of Artillery.
Lieutenant-Colonel (temporary) Robert ELLIOT, D.S.O. (38618), Royal Regiment of Artillery (Camberley).
Lieutenant-Colonel (temporary) Alan James Wroughton MACLEOD, D.S.O. (I.A.377), 12th Frontier Force Regiment, Indian Army.
Lieutenant-Colonel (temporary) Derek Gordon Thomond HORSFORD, D.S.O. (I.A.769), 8th Gurkha Rifles, Indian Army.

The Distinguished Service Order.

Major-General (acting) William Alfred DIMOLINE, C.B.E., M.C. (12248), late Royal Corps of Signals (Wirral, Cheshire).
Brigadier (temporary) Henry Sackville Joynt BOURKE, O.B.E., M.C. (18637), Royal Regiment of Artillery (Netley).
Brigadier (acting) Averall John DANIELL, M.B.E. (26961), Royal Regiment of Artillery (Camberley).
Colonel (acting) Harry Clifford Blakemore HALL (17664), Royal Regiment of Artillery (Beaconsfield).
Lieutenant-Colonel (temporary) Geoffrey Russell ARMSTRONG, M.C. (65394), Royal Regiment of Artillery (London, E.C.4).
Lieutenant-Colonel (temporary) John Bruce CHAPLIN (53626), Royal Regiment of Artillery.
Lieutenant-Colonel (acting) Leslie William George JENKINS (70748), Royal Regiment of Artillery (Drewsteignton).
Lieutenant-Colonel (temporary) Basil Joseph LEECH (34837), The Royal Northumberland Fusiliers (Newcastle-on-Tyne).
Lieutenant-Colonel (temporary) Frank Job GOULSON (66499), The Lincolnshire Regiment (attd. The Gold Coast Regiment) (Felixstowe).
Lieutenant-Colonel (temporary) Gretton Francis FOSTER, M.C. (217359), The Suffolk Regiment (Coggeshall, Sussex).
Lieutenant-Colonel (acting) William Peter Bertram ARKWRIGHT (47516), The Royal Scots Fusiliers (Okehampton).
Lieutenant-Colonel (temporary) Oliver Geoffrey Woodhouse WHITE (47671), The Dorsetshire Regiment (Farnborough, Hants.).
Lieutenant-Colonel (temporary) Harold du Pre FINCH (28069), The Royal Berkshire Regiment (Princess Charlotte of Wales's) (Warminster).
Major (temporary) Francis Hugh Briggs BOSHELL (112813), The Royal Berkshire Regiment (Princess Charlotte of Wales's) (London, W.5).
Brigadier (temporary) Charles Roger Alan SWYNNERTON (438), The North Staffordshire Regiment (The Prince of Wales's) (Church Crookham).
Brigadier (temporary) Abdy Henry Gough RICKETTS, O.B.E. (33748), The Durham Light Infantry (Camberley).
Lieutenant-Colonel (temporary) Lewis Balfour OATTS (20057), The Highland Light Infantry (City of Glasgow Regiment) (attd. The Chin Rifles) (Penirink, Midlothian).
Major (temporary) John Stuart Frederick Andres Forbes BURNETT, M.C. (162694), The Argyll and Sutherland Highlanders (Princess Louise's) (Newrachar, Aberdeenshire).
Lieutenant-Colonel (temporary) Frederick PALTRIDGE (59675), General List (Res. of Off.) (Dublin).
Major (temporary) Alister Henry CAMPBELL, M.C. (I.A.859), 7th Light Cavalry, Indian Armoured Corps.
Lieutenant-Colonel (acting) George Hannyngton CARR, M.B.E. (I.A.169), The Royal Deccan Horse (9th Horse), Indian Armoured Corps.
Lieutenant-Colonel (temporary) James Ronald KERR, M.A., M.B., B.Ch. (MZ.15370), Indian Medical Service.
Lieutenant-Colonel (temporary) Ian Connaill Athos LAUDER (I.A.805), 5th Mahratta Light Infantry, Indian Army.
Lieutenant-Colonel (acting) George Edgar PARKER, M.B.E., M.C. (EC.9368), 6th Rajputana Rifles, Indian Army.
Lieutenant-Colonel (temporary) William Hubert BARLOW-WHEELER (I.A.84), 11th Sikh Regiment, Indian Army.
Lieutenant-Colonel (temporary) Hubert George CONROY, M.C. (I.A.689), 15th Punjab Regiment, Indian Army.
Brigadier (acting) James Francis Robert FORMAN (I.A.890), 19th Hyderabad Regiment, Indian Army.
Lieutenant-Colonel (acting) Robert John O'LONE (I.A.122), 3rd Queen Alexandra's Own Gurkha Rifles, Indian Army.
Lieutenant-Colonel (temporary) Walter Colyear WALKER (I.A.214), 8th Gurkha Rifles, Indian Army.
Lieutenant-Colonel (temporary) Drummond David Maurice MCREADY, O.B.E. (I.A.223), 10th Gurkha Rifles, Indian Army.

Bar to the Military Cross.

Major (temporary) Thomas Edward DIMSDALE, M.C. (53113), 3rd Carabiniers (The Prince of Wales's Dragoon Guards), Royal Armoured Corps (Burtingford).
Major (temporary) Cecil Gerald MERTON, M.C. (189643), General List (attd. The Burma Rifles).
Captain (temporary) MOHAMMED JAMSHED, M.C. (EC.3302), 1st Punjab Regiment, Indian Army.
Major (temporary) Richard Frederick JOLLEY, M.C. (EC.7052), 2nd Punjab Regiment, Indian Army.
Major (temporary) Alastair Henry Johnstone DUNLOP, M.C. (I.A.872), 4th Bombay Grenadiers, Indian Army.
Subadar-Major RAGHUBIR THAPA, M.C. (7945.I.O.), 8th Gurkha Rifles, Indian Army.
Major (temporary) William Archibald GOLDBERG, M.C. (EC.5850), Indian Intelligence Corps.

The Military Cross.

Major (temporary) Arthur John BAYLEY (134841), Royal Armoured Corps (Croydon).
Major (temporary) Peter Walter CRAIG (113067), Royal Armoured Corps (Aberdeen).
Captain (acting) Hugh BAKER (187147), Royal Armoured Corps (Portsmouth).
Lieutenant George Gordon BUCKLEY (155894), Royal Armoured Corps (New Ferry, Cheshire).

Gazette 17.1.46. (*The London Gazette*)

Bibliography

Carmichael, Pat, *Mountain Battery* (Bournemouth: Devin Books, 1983).

Duckett, Richard *The Special Operations Executive in Burma* (London: Bloomsbury Academic, 2017).

Evans, Lieutenant-General Sir Geoffrey KBE, CB, DSO *The Johnnies* (London: Cassell, 1964).

Fergusson, Bernard, Brigadier *The Wild Green Earth* (London: Collins 1946).

Lunt, Major General J D, *The Burma Rifles: Journal of the Society for Army Historical Research. Vol. 76, No. 307*

Lunt, Major General J D, *The Retreat from Burma 1941-1945* (Newton Abbot: David & Charles Publishing 1986).

McDonald Fraser, George, *Safely Quartered Out Here* (London: Harper Collins, 1992).

Slim, Field Marshall Viscount, *Defeat into Victory* (London: Cassell, 1956).

Smyth, Sir John, *Before the Dawn* (London: Cassell, 1957).